HELL RANCH

RANCH

The Nightmare Tale of Voodoo, Drugs, & Death in Matamoros

Clifford L. Linedecker

DIAMOND BOOKS ★ Austin, Texas

For Junko and the Vaughans, Don and Nan —
for sharing hectic days and sleepless nights.

All photos courtesy of The Houston Post

Author's Note

North Americans not of Spanish or Indian descent may have difficulty, as I once did, deciphering the Mexican and Cuban names in this story.

It will be helpful to note that among Hispanics, the family name — that of the father — appears immediately after the given names. And the family name is followed by the maiden name, or family name of the mother. Thus, on second reference, the Federal Judicial Police commander of the Matamoros district, Juan Benitez Ayala, for example, becomes Benitez. Speaking or writing the family name of both the father and mother is permissable usage on second references as well, thus the commander can also be referred to as Benitez Ayala.

FIRST EDITION

Copyright © 1989
By Clifford L. Linedecker

Published in the United States of America
By Diamond Books
An Imprint of Eakin Publications, Inc.
P.O. Drawer 90159   ★   Austin, TX 78709-0159

ISBN 0-89015-734-0

Contents

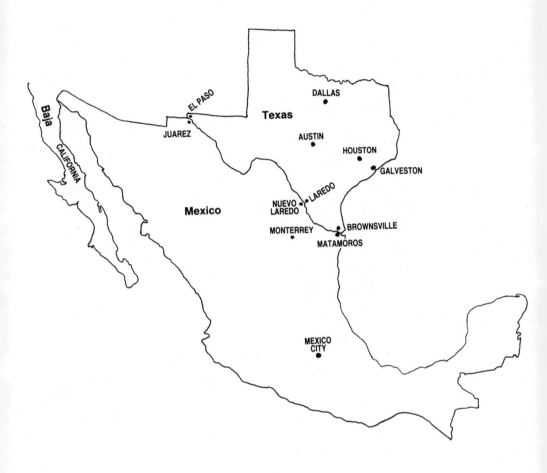

Acknowledgments

Books are neither conceived nor born by and of themselves. The efforts of several people working in concert with the individuals eventually credited as the authors are necessary to creation and completion of the projects.

Some of the people who gave of their time, ideas, and abilities to help make this book a reality, and to whom I owe a debt of gratitude, are:

My publisher, Tony Seidl, for phoning me and saying: "Have I got a book for you."

My editor, Jim Connor, for bringing organization to disorganization, and undertaking a difficult task under pressure to provide a thoroughly sparkling and professional backup job that kept the book accurate, literate, and readable.

To Jan Tomas and her border brigade, for ferreting out elusive information, tying down facts, and helping sort out intricacies of the Spanish language and the Mexican mind that were so confusing to an Anglo writer from the Midwest.

To American expatriot journalists and freelancers in Mexico City and elsewhere in Mexico, for responding to pleas for help tracking down leads and attending press conferences.

The assistance of all those in Texas and Mexico who helped in the collecting of information and the cutting through of a confusing tangle of language differences and bureaucratic confusion, made it possible to speed the delivery of the completed manuscript by many weeks.

Finally, thanks go to my friend and colleague, Billy Burt, for blurting out the title, *Hell Ranch,* after I had scribbled dozens of lesser suggestions.

Introduction

Even those who feared the worst, when American pre-med student Mark Kilroy mysteriously vanished during a Spring Break night out in Matamoros, Mexico, with his college pals, never suspected the staggering magnitude of the horror that had claimed him.

There was no way of knowing that the search for the twenty-one-year-old American boy-next-door would eventually uncover a macabre blood cult whose hunger for drug riches would lead to a nightmare journey into black magic, perversion and human sacrifice engineered by the son of Cuban immigrants to the U.S. named Adolfo de Jesus Constanzo.

Blood cults, and misused mysticism twisted and utilized for evil gain aren't new to Mexico. Our neighbor to the south is especially steeped in superstition and a spiritual intensity that seems to make it uniquely prone to abuse by madmen and charlatans who manipulate belief in the preternatural and religious faith for their own selfish ends.

Of course, the United States has had its share of confidence men and lunatics who misuse religious belief, and twist the confused spirituality of the naive to serve their needs. The mad Hoosier preacher, Jim Jones, lured hundreds of the desperate poor to Guyana with his People's Temple, where they lost their lives in a perverted orgy of suicide and murder. And more recently the U.S. has been the ferocious internal bloodletting that has devastated the International Society for Krishna Consciousness, popularly known as the Hare Krishna movement. Bodies of Hare Krishnas and former Krishna devotees were littered across the country.

But Mexico had already earned an especially bloody footnote in the history of gruesome cult and serial murders in the early 1960s, with the outrageous crimes of brothers Santos and Cayetano Hernandez and their prostitute priestess Magdalena Solis; and with the perverted performance of sisters Delfina and Maria de Jesus Gonzales.

Ironically, the method of operation and the profile of the crimes committed by the Hernandez brothers and their sinister priestess, have certain striking similarities to the evils blamed on Constanzo that were uncovered early in 1989 in Matamoros. Like Constanzo, the Hernandez brothers and Magdalena formed a cult that incorporated human sacrifice into its religious rites. Both cults operated in the Mexican state of Tamaulipas; the leadership of both were dominated by homosexuals; and some of the leaders shared the same family name, Hernandez.

Santos and Cayetano Hernandez formed their cult early in 1963 in the poor village of Yerba Buena, by convincing local farmers that mountain gods would reward them with great riches if they worshipped with proper piety and offered unselfish sacrifices. At first the only sacrifice required by the gods was sex with the brothers — the women with Santos, and the men with Cayetano.

But after months of sex, with no sign of the promised treasure, the worshippers were becoming discontented. So the brothers journeyed to Monterrey, in the adjoining state of Nuevo Leon, where they found Magdalena, an attractive blonde prostitute, and her brother, Eleazor Solis, who was also her pimp. The brother and sister, both homosexual, agreed to the Hernandez's hastily outlined scheme to return to the village and pose as the gods of the mountains.

After several more weeks of sexual communing with the gods and the high priests — and still no treasure — the faithful villagers were becoming restless again. So they were advised that the gods demanded a human sacrifice. The two most doubting villagers were brutally beaten to death by their neighbors, and their blood drunk from ceremonial bowls. During the next few weeks, six others who had carelessly expressed doubts about the legitimacy of the gods, were also sacrificed.

The scam fell apart when a teenage beauty who had been relinquished by Santos to the velvety arms of the goddess, began slipping away from Magdalena for stolen romantic moments with her former priest lover. Magdalena exploded angrily when she learned of the blasphemy, and announced that the fickle teenager must be sacrificed.

The terrified girl was tied to a cross, knocked unconscious by the raging lesbian, and beaten to death by the remaining villagers still faithful to the priests and their gods. But a fourteen-year-old boy who was not one of the cultists, saw the worshippers piling brush around the girl's body, and light it. As he watched in horror, they used machetes to hack to death another farmer who was pointed out as a doubter by Magdalena. The boy hurried to the next town and told police what he had seen.

Police were skeptical of the story. A patrolman eventually consented to drive to the mountain lair of the cultists to check out the story. The policeman and the boy were never seen alive again. When a squad of police sent from Ciudad Victoria, the capital city of Tamaulipas, drove to the village to look for the missing duo they found their horribly mutilated bodies. The policeman's heart had been ripped from his chest.

Rifle fire greeted the policemen when they approached the caves where the cultists were holed up, and three officers were wounded. But the firepower and the odds were against the cultists, and the shootout quickly ended with their surrender. Police found Santos Hernandez shot to death. His brother, Cayetano, was missing, and it was sometime before investigators learned he had been murdered by another cultist who wanted to replace him as a priest. Magdalena, her brother, and twelve other cultists surrendered, and were quickly put on trial and sentenced to long prison terms.

The murderous Gonzales sisters didn't pretend to be in communion with the gods. They were ruthless white slavers and brothel keepers, who killed or ordered the slaying of more than eighty girls and young women. Several newborn babies, and at least eleven men murdered for their pay (after stopping at the sisters' brothels with money earned as migratory workers in the United States) were also found buried at the ranch. The men's drinks were drugged, and when they passed out they were garrotted, stabbed, or beaten to death.

Many of the girls were lured into the clutches of the remorseless sisters by newspaper advertisements with the promise of jobs as domestics to young women. Once ushered into the brothels, their fate was sealed. The girls were repeatedly beaten and raped during a "break-in" period, then deliberately hooked on drugs such as heroin or cocaine. They worked in the brothels until their youth and usefulness was gone. Then the sisters ordered them murdered, to be replaced by younger, fresher girls.

Prostitutes who became pregnant were hung by their wrists and beaten on the stomach until they aborted. If the mother lived, she was put back to work as soon as she could sit up. If she died, she was buried in the crude ossuary that surrounded the brothel.

The sisters wreaked their misery on a spread in the small central Mexican state of Guanajuato north of Mexico City, called the Rancho El Angel. After more than ten terrible years, police finally broke up the prostitution and murder ring in 1963.

The cult murders in Tamaulipas state, and the slaughter at the Angel Ranch were dreadful. But I've written before about dreadful murders, and the mindless brutality of carefully planned, organized homicide. When I began this project there was no way of knowing that the slaughter in Matamoros and Mexico City would come to stand out in singular wretchedness from all the others.

During more than thirty-years as a daily newspaper journalist, editor, freelancer, and author I've investigated and written about serial killers; about the degeneracy, heartbreak and violence of the narcotics trade and drug abuse; and about the quixotic lure of strange religious cults.

I posed as a workman to enter the home of John Wayne Gacy, Jr., who raped, tortured and slaughtered at least thirty-three young men and boys, and then buried most of them under his house on the outskirts of Chicago.

I rode on a bus from Philadelphia to the former federal drug treatment center at Lexington, Kentucky, with a desperate teenager who was committing herself to the program there in a last ditch effort to kick a heroin habit because dealers and pimps were trying to turn her into a prostitute. And I covered the story a few weeks later when her body was found in the doorway of a South Street ghetto bar. She had beaten me back to Philadelphia, and was dead of an overdose.

I have attended a convention in Minneapolis of Witches, sorcerers, and black magicians; worshipped with pagans at coven meetings in Philadelphia, Chicago, and Indiana; shared vegetarian meals with Hare Krishnas; chanted with Sufis; attended lectures by followers of the Church Universal and Triumphant; tramped through woods in Michigan's Upper Peninsula looking for UFOs with men and women who insisted they communed with Space Intelligences; argued theological esoterics with ominous, black-robed acolytes of the Process; and commiserated with a Satanist who was worried that the courts would take away visitation rights with his daughter because he kept a tombstone in his home with his ex-wife's name chiseled on it.

And I have attended mystical ceremonies conducted in Chicago by a *Santeria* priestess, who blew smoke from strong Cuban cigars and spit eye-stinging sprays of cheap, potent rum over an altar while petitioning favors and protection from gods summoned from ancient Africa. She was unpopular among the Afro-Caribbean religion's purists because she was an animal lover who refused to spill blood — and thus was not accepted as a true *Santera*. The gods demanded blood sacrifice.

But nothing prepared me for the utterly ruthless brutality and degeneracy of the crimes blamed on Adolfo de Jesus Constanzo and his followers. In an area already notorious for savagery and violence, his crimes horrified even veteran police officers.

The abominations committed at the Santa Elena Ranch, just south of the American border at Brownsville, Texas, seemed to be too nauseating to contemplate. But even those atrocities didn't represent the full scale of Constanzo's wretchedness. He and his cohorts had been conducting their reign of terror in Mexico City where he dumped a grisly scattering of mutilated and dismembered bodies on the streets, in parks and in rivers for at least eighteen-months before expanding his operation to the border area.

As I probed further into the malignant behavior of the Rasputin-like character whose followers called him *El Padrino*, — Godfather — I learned that he had incorporated the worst possible elements of the serial killer, of the narcotics trafficker, and of blood cultists into a single evil endeavor.

When the slaughter at the Santa Elena Ranch was first uncovered, news reports talked of cannibalism and dreadful Satanic rites. Constanzo was neither a cannibal, nor a Satanist. But he was truly demonic. He was a thoroughly ruthless and malevolent genius with a messianic ability to command the loyalty and blind obedience of followers who joined him, zombie-like, in a loathsome blood feast of dope dealing, terror, torture, and human sacrifice.

It all started to come apart when a quartet of former high-school chums from Texas got together in Matamoros for a night on the town during their college Spring Break.

Mark Kilroy

Bradley Moore, Brent Martin, and Bill Huddleston

CHAPTER 1

A Disappearance

IT WAS NEARLY 2:00 A.M. on Tuesday, March 14, and Mark Kilroy; was feeling good. The twenty-one-year-old premed student from the University of Texas at Austin had spent the evening drinking with his best friends in one hot Mexican bar after another, and the alcohol was giving him a definite buzz.

Less than thirteen hours later, Mark Kilroy would be dead.

The reason for the boys' celebration was Spring Break 1989, a week-long vacation from the rigors and responsibilities of college. It was something for which Mark and his buddies — Bradley Moore and Brent Martin, both twenty, and twenty-one-year-old Bill Huddleston — had planned the entire fall semester. In fact, spring break and everything that came with it — beer, partying, Miss Tanline contests and fun on the beach — was just about the only topic of conversation whenever the boys got in touch by phone.

The four caballeros had met while attending high school in their home town of Santa Fe, Texas, a few miles from Houston. Mark, Bradley, and Brent had played basketball, and Mark and Bill played baseball. And though they eventually ended up at different colleges after graduation — Bradley was a third-year electrical engineering major at Texas A&M-College Station; Bill a junior at Texas A&M-Galveston, and Brent was a sophomore at Alvin Community College — their friendship had remained strong and committed.

The group's original spring break destination was South Padre Island, Texas, a jumping vacation mecca deep in the Lower Rio Grande Valley that appeals to older Texas tourists and, during spring break, to thousands of college kids who have neither the time, money nor inclination to travel to Florida.

The area is noted in travel guides for its beautiful white beaches, fine fishing and towering sand dunes, but during spring break there are other attractions. To the eager college students who save and scheme for a few days of fun in the sun, bottomless bottles of beer and daily bikini contests are far more enticing than scenic sand dunes, golf courses or wildlife refuges.

Fort Lauderdale and Daytona Beach, Florida, get most of the spring break coverage on MTV, but over the years South Padre Island and, to a lesser degree, the nearby bordertown of Brownsville, have become popular springtime havens for college students looking for action.

Consequently, South Padre Island has become a gold mine for shrewd entrepreneurs who make their living by catering to young people in a party mood. Major beer companies sponsor traditional spring break activities such as Miss Tanline contests, teeny bikini competitions, free telephone calls home and even surf-simulator rides for students too timid to try the real thing at the beach.

To Mark and his pals, these activities, not to mention the tanned and slender girls sure to be parading around in skimpy bikinis, were just the thing to take their minds off books and academics. Mark and Bradley had made the trip to South Padre Island the year before, although not as a team.

Bradley was the first to finish his final exams, and on Friday, began his spring break by driving his Mustang from his mobile home in Bryan to the UT Austin campus to pick up Mark at his dorm. From there, the two friends drove to Santa Fe, where they were to meet up with Bill and Brent.

On the trip, they caught up with what had happened during the previous semester and talked about spring break and the coming summer in Santa Fe. Their conversation had a tone of finality to it, because the boys realized that this would probably be the last summer they would spend together. The end of Bradley's college days was approaching, and Mark, a junior working for a bachelors degree in bio-chemistry, was bearing down on his studies so he could graduate with good marks and continue his education in medical school. New responsibilities were rapidly approaching, and summer fun at South Padre Island, unfortunately, probably wouldn't be part of them.

Around midnight, the four boys piled into Brent's more spacious Cutlass and started out along the winding Texas coastline that would eventually lead them to South Padre Island. Heavy fog kept their speed down, and the trip took nearly nine hours. By the time they arrived, it was mid-morning and the group was ready to party.

The Sheraton Hotel where they were staying had prepared for the influx of college students like a well-led army preparing for battle. Unnecessary furniture had been removed from the lobby, and anything breakable was relocated to a safer spot. The hotels on South Padre Island love spring breakers — they bring a lot of money to the local economy — but college students primed with beer and youthful exuberance, can be destructive, clumsy and careless. And broken furniture is costly to replace. At every hotel on the island, the motto during spring break is the same: Better safe than sorry.

Mark, Bill, Brent, and Bradley couldn't care less about the hotel they were booked in. They had driven all night for only three things — the beach, beer, and bikinied babes — and they didn't want to waste any time in finding them. After checking in, they showered, wolfed down a fast meal and hit the beach looking for action.

And that's exactly what they found. Although the big crowds had yet to arrive, South Padre Island was already alive with thousands of excited college students from nearly every state. Dozens of exciting events and organizations — including one Christian group that had driven all the way from Madison, Wisconsin, to distribute pamphlets, suntan lotion and pleas to "pray rather than party" — vied for the boys' attention. Over here was a bevy of bikini-clad gals competing for titles that would make their mothers blush, while over there beer companies pushed free movies, free concerts, and just about everything else except free brew.

The boys took advantage of everything the massive beach party had to offer. Mark and Bradley used the free phone lines to call home to let their parents know they had arrived safely. They caught some rays on the beach, and partied until dawn the following day with some girls from Indiana's Purdue University who were sharing the room next door.

As the weekend progressed, the group established a routine that allowed them to make the most of their vacation. They visited the beach early in the morning to work on their tans and scope the women, then after lunch they would trek behind the Sheraton and watch the daily Miss Tanline contests. The participants were sure to show some forbidden skin, and the crowds cheered wildly for the coed who proved to be the most recklessly daring. Police warned the sponsors frequently about the nudity, but graciously turned their backs when off-limits body parts were "accidentally" exposed. The boys couldn't get enough, and the contests were one of the highlights of their day.

In the late afternoon the weary quartet would return to their hotel rooms to catch a little sleep, although they seldom managed more than an hour or two. Then, during dinner they would debate plans for the evening.

The rousing Mexican border town of Matamoros was only a short drive away, and its lure was strong. The boys had heard about the pretty girls, cheap drinks and party atmosphere from others who had been there, and Sunday evening they decided to check it out for themselves.

Before leaving, they ate a relaxing dinner at the Sonic Drive-In in nearby Port Isabel, where they met some girls from the University of Kansas who were also planning a trip across the border. The group decided to caravan, and the girls followed Brent's car the twenty-four miles to the Brownsville-Matamoros international cross-over.

The two groups parked their cars next to each other on the American side of the Rio Grande and walked across the international bridge that led to Matamoros, Brownsville's sister city to the south.

One of the largest and most prosperous cities in northern Mexico, Matamoros supports a population of more than 180,000. During spring break, however, the population explodes as American college kids — most of them too young to drink at home — flee the restrictive rules of home into the eager arms of a city that has no minimum drinking age. In Matamoros, as with most large Mexican cities, if you have the money, you can buy a beer and a fresh lime for one dollar — and almost anything else you want.

Indeed, Matamoros, warm, dusty and Mexican in every sense of the word, welcomes every North American visitor it can get, especially American college students with extra money to spend. Like South Padre Island, tourism is one of the city's largest industries, and the thousands of college students who visit each year mean millions of pesos for the cantinas, restaurants, and nightclubs that cater to their desire to party.

Their first night in Matamoros was uneventful. The students spent most of the evening drinking chilled bottles of Corona, chatting and flirting in a popular bar called Sgt. Pepper's, before the girls left to sight-see and party on their own.

After leaving Sgt. Pepper's, Mark, Bradley, Brent, and Bill cruised Avenida Alvaro Obregon, the area's main tourist drag. They visited several other jam-packed bars, shot the bull with fellow students and generally did their best to forget classes and schoolbooks. At the end of the evening, the four friends drove back to South Padre Island and their rooms at the Sheraton where they slumped wearily into bed, a little drunk and very tired.

The following Monday the Spring Break ritual was resumed. The boys hit the beach first, had lunch, then soaked up the party atmosphere. Mark had a long chat with one of the girls in the day's Miss Tanline contest, a pretty coed from Southwest Texas State University. Later in the evening the four pals dropped by a condo party hosted by some of Mark's former fraternity buddies from his two years at Tarleton State University in Stephenville. He had attended Tarleton State on an athletic scholarship before transferring to the University of Texas-Austin to pursue his premed major.

About 10:30, the party started to drag, and the boys decided to make another trek to Matamoros. The drive went quickly, and they again parked on the Brownsville side of the border.

By this time the major rush of spring breakers had arrived, and Avenida Alvaro Obregon and the rest of Matamoros's shopping and business district was crammed with screaming, sweating and hard-drinking college students. Official estimates put the night's crowd at nearly 15,000, and pale Anglo bodies outnumbered the brown-skinned natives as they filled almost every stool in every bar in town. Party-crazed students without stools, having no where else to go, spilled out the doors and into the city's hot, dirty streets, where the celebrating continued. The streets were alive with the crush of students, drinking, dancing and yelling to the ear-splitting throb of rock, Tex-Mex, and country-western music that spilled outside from bands and jukeboxes in the bars.

In an effort to beat the dense crowds, the boys looked for the bar with the shortest line. They selected a loud, neon-illuminated club called Los Sombreros. After downing a couple of Coronas there, the group pushed further into the mass of students that all but enveloped the border town's nightclub district, eventually winding up at the London Pub. Only it wasn't called the London Pub during spring break. In an effort to add to its appeal with the students, the joint had been temporarily renamed the Hardrock Cafe.

The Hardrock Cafe was even louder and more raucous than Los Sombreros, and the boys stood at the bar, screaming and hooting as spring breakers on the balcony tossed empty beer cans at the crowd below.

Mark, usually one of the more shy members of the foursome, began talking with some girls, and after awhile he left the group for a while to party on his own. About 2:00 A.M., Bill suggested they head back to the hotel, and they found Mark outside the bar chatting up the beauty from the Miss Tanline contest.

Their destination was the international bridge only a couple of blocks away, alive with the hum of tires from a bumper-to-bumper string of cars and trucks, and brightly lighted traffic lanes. But the narrow streets were overflowing with loud students walking and staggering in varying stages of drunkenness. What should have been a fifteen-minute stroll took much longer. Bradley and Brent walked point for the group and were quickly swallowed by the flood of people heading toward the U.S. side of the border.

Mark stopped in front of a private residence to say goodbye to the girl from the Miss Tanline contest. When Bill caught up with him, Mark told his friend that he didn't look very good. Bill reassured Mark that he was merely tired. It had been a long day and night of partying. Mark appeared to accept that explanation. Then Bill asked him to wait while he looked for an alley or corner where he could relieve himself of some of the beer he had consumed that night.

When Bill returned a couple of minutes later, Mark was nowhere to be found. Puzzled, Bill looked around for a few moments, then quickly caught up with Bradley and Brent in front of a tourist-trap souvenir shop called Garcia's just down the road from the international bridge. But Mark wasn't with them and they hadn't seen him.

Bill was a little foggy from the alcohol and near non-stop partying, but he vaguely recalled noticing a Mexican man standing on a shadowy corner calling to Mark in English. The Mexican asked something like, "Didn't I just meet you somewhere?," or "Do you want a ride?" Bill glimpsed Mark cautiously approach the stranger, who was standing next to a red pickup truck. But when Bill returned from his comfort stop a couple of minutes later, both Mark and the mysterious stranger had vanished.

Bill, Bradley, and Brent crossed the bridge to their car, hoping to find Mark waiting inside. He wasn't there. The concern of Mark's buddies was mounting, and they returned to Matamoros where they combed the thinning streets looking for him until about 4:00 A.M. The bars had emptied long ago, and the streets were quiet. Mark seemed to have disappeared without a trace. No one saw him leave, and no one except Bill could remember seeing the strange man or his red pickup truck. The trio reluctantly gave up their search, and returned to their car. The drive back to South Padre Island was subdued, and the boys talked hopefully of finding Mark back in their hotel room. Perhaps, they mused, he had caught a ride with someone else.

Mark wasn't in the hotel room. And when his buddies awakened from fitful sleep a few hours later, and he still hadn't returned, they telephoned his parents. Immigration authorities, then police in Matamoros and Brownsville were also notified that the American college student was missing.

A missing tourist is not an uncommon occurrence in a city the size of Matamoros, especially during spring break when the city swells with celebrating American students. The rowdy kids cause their share of problems, and the city's police force usually has its hands full with drug deals gone bad, bar fights and other troubles that accompany young people in large numbers.

But Mark Kilroy was not like most college students. He was intelligent and healthy. He placed fourteenth in his 1986 high school graduating class of 210 students, and won a basketball scholarship to Tarleton College. He gave up the scholarship after two years and transferred to the University of Texas so he could concentrate on his studies. He didn't experiment with drugs. He was a responsible student and a loving son — definitely not the type to suddenly walk off unannounced and disappear on his own volition, deliberately leaving family and friends to worry about him.

Mark's disappearance made no sense to his friends or his family. They quickly contacted authorities on both sides of the border and insisted a search for the missing college student begin.

Unlike many missing person reports filed in a Mexican border town, this one wasn't going to rest uninvestigated and forgotten in the bottom of a file cabinet. James and Helen Kilroy were determined to find their eldest son.

The search for Mark was continuous by the family and friends.

Flyers regarding Marks disappearance were posted and yellow ribbons were tied to express everyone's concern.

CHAPTER 2

The Search for Mark Kilroy

JAMES AND HELEN KILROY were horrified at the news of their oldest son's disappearance, but they didn't panic. During the first thirty-six hours they felt confident that Mark would reappear unharmed, perhaps in a Mexican jail, and they passed the time by talking on the phone with officials in Brownsville and with the boys who were with Mark the night he vanished.

The U.S. consul in Matamoros was contacted for help, and arrangements were made to have Mark's photo and description circulated at local jails, hospitals, and bars.

But when Mark still hadn't shown up by March 16, his family began to fear the worst. On the advice of investigators in Brownsville, James Kilroy, a chemical engineer, headed to Matamoros with Eddie de la Houssaye, a friend, to pass out flyers and talk with residents. Mark's mother stayed home and manned the telephone along with concerned neighbors.

At her side was Bill Huddleston's mother, Gwen. Realizing that the best way to bring Mark home was to make his disappearance public, she contacted the media and asked them to spread the word. Newspapers and television stations jumped at the chance. The story of an American college student missing in Mexico was news.

As the days passed with no new information, the Kilroys put increasing pressure on American and Mexican officials to find their son.

Initially, authorities in Matamoros insisted that the search should be focused on Brownsville and South Texas. They said that preliminary investigation indicated he had crossed the international bridge into the U.S. before disappearing. Matamoros's fragile tourist industry didn't need negative publicity about a young college boy disappearing there during spring break.

But evidence, especially Bill Huddleston's ominous first-person account of Mark's brush with the mysterious young Mexican along the Avenida Alvaro Obregon, was just too strong to place the premed student anywhere except in Matamoros when he dropped from sight. Cameron County Sheriff's investigators, in Brownsville, Brownsville police, and agents with other American law enforcement agencies were convinced that Mexico was the place to look for the missing youth.

Meanwhile, Gwen Huddleston, whose studio in Santa Fe teaches dance, music, baton twirling, gymnastics and karate, temporarily turned her business over to other managers in order to help the Kilroys search for Mark. She and Helen Kilroy kept the story of Mark's mysterious disappearance alive with frequent updates to area newspapers and television stations and by making themselves as accessible as possible to local reporters. However, the agonizing wait quickly became too much for Helen Kilroy and she eventually joined her husband in Brownsville.

One of the first American officials to be contacted by the Kilroys was Oran Neck, Jr., a street-wise and savvy U.S. Customs chief headquartered in Brownsville, Texas. As a native of the city, Neck was familiar with the workings of American-Mexican border towns and their curious symbiotic relationship. He knew the people and the way of life on the border and he understood the two divergent cultures as few Americans ever could.

The Kilroys trusted Neck, and as the search for Mark continued, they inherently realized that whatever he told them was the truth. Neck, in turn, came to admire the Kilroys — a Catholic family with deep religious beliefs — for the strength and character they showed during such a difficult period in their lives.

He admittedly became emotionally involved in the case. Neck and the Kilroys became close friends.

As the days turned into weeks, the Kilroys and a select group of friends became fixtures in the Brownsville-Matamoros area. They saturated the Mexican city and the Lower Rio Grande Valley with more than 20,000 fliers carrying Mark's picture and information about his disappearance. The Kilroys also offered a $5,000 reward, later raised to $15,000 thanks to contributions from friends and townfolk, for information on Mark's whereabouts or fate.

At the same time, Mexican police and American Customs agents were questioning a large number of people on both sides of the border about Mark's disappearance. But few of the interviews produced any useful information. It was almost as if the college junior had literally been yanked from the face of the earth.

It's difficult enough to find a missing person when he disappears in his native country, but the task becomes doubly hard when the search involves two countries — even nations as close as Mexico and the United States. Such a search brings with it bureaucratic, territorial and cultural problems that can hinder efforts and waste precious time.

Neck and Cameron County (Texas) Chief Investigator George Gavito knew the Kilroys needed some extra help in the search for their son, and they worked quickly to clear the red tape clogging the pipeline between U.S. and

Mexican law enforcement agencies. "Good people like that deserve a break," Neck was later quoted by journalists. "You can't turn your back on them."

The Kilroys refused to return to their home in Santa Fe during the initial stages of the search for Mark, and they visited the Cameron County sheriff's office so frequently that they came to know the secretaries there by name.

Everyone who met the distressed couple during the search for Mark perceived them fondly as loving parents who faced the crisis with unwavering strength and resolve. "They always seemed to be such wonderful people," R. C. Williams, senior chief deputy at the Cameron county sheriff's office, told the *San Antonio Light*. "They worked so hard. They did everything humanly possible to find their son."

Even television got into the act when the Fox Network's popular "America's Most Wanted" series featured a reenactment of what police officials believed happened to Mark Kilroy on the night of March 14. The program also showed a picture of Mark and a telephone number for people who might have information. More than ninety people phoned in with potential tips and words of encouragement.

And host Maury Povich on television's popular, "A Current Affair," interviewed Mark's chums about their fateful night on the town in Matamoros, and the popular premed student's perplexing disappearance.

But none of the publicity produced any solid leads. The effort put into the search for Mark appeared to be in vain. Weeks passed with no new information about Mark or his whereabouts, although U.S. and Mexican authorities received several tips that the missing student was being held at various locations in and around Matamoros. Unfortunately, those rumors all turned out to be false, and the Kilroys found their hopes being cruelly raised then dashed to the ground.

In a bizarre turn of events, a psychic told police she had a vision in which she saw Mark Kilroy's body lying next to what appeared to be a witch's cauldron. And a self-proclaimed satanist told police he had killed the college student and buried his body along a lonely stretch of beach. However, he quickly recanted his story under hard questioning by police.

As their options began, one after another, to disintegrate, the Kilroys made impassioned pleas to any politician who would listen. Texas congressman Lloyd Criss agreed to help the Kilroys, and he arranged a meeting with State Attorney General Jim Mattox, who in turn contacted the Tamaulipas, Mexico, state attorney general's office.

"Their persistence got everybody involved in this case," Elma Christopher, a spokeswoman for Mattox, told the *Houston Chronicle*. "They made very loving feelings known about their son and very rational pleas for help."

The Kilroys also contacted San Antonio Mayor Henry Cisneros, who was widely admired by Mexicans and who, conveniently enough, happened to have roomed with Mexico President Carlos Salinas de Gortari while attending Harvard University.

At the Kilroy's request, the mayor traveled across the border to meet with the mayors of Matamoros and Brownsville. He expressed his concern for the border region and encouraged the Mexican police and U.S. Customs agents to work together in finding Mark. He spotlighted the concern of Mexican officials about the effect of the search on tourism at a joint press conference in Brownsville with Matamoros Mayor Fernando Montemayor Lozano and Brownsville Mayor Ygnacio Garza: "This is an important case, and it should not reflect in any way on Brownsville, Matamoros of Mexico as a place of vacation."

Cisneros' hopeful cheerleading wasn't much help, but the Kilroys felt that any help in the search for Mark — especially from a prominent politician like Cisneros — had to be beneficial.

Despite their courageous resolve, the ordeal took a heavy emotional toll on James and Helen Kilroy and the law enforcement agencies working valiantly to find their son. As the search dragged on, James Kilroy admitted that his heart sank a little more with every passing day, and he tried to prepare himself for accepting Mark's loss if he was not found alive.

But the Kilroys and Mark's nineteen-year-old brother, Keith, refused to give up hope, and they found much comfort in their deep religious faith. Because they were spending so much time in Brownsville, the family started attending services at St. Luke's Catholic Church and spending time with the church's popular and gregarious priest, Father Juan Nicolau. Despite their hectic schedule, the Kilroys found time every day to drop by St. Luke's to say a prayer for their missing son and to receive words of encouragement from Father Nicolau.

Touched by the Kilroys' plight, the people of Brownsville took the family into their hearts, showering them with warmth and offers of help. Helen Kilroy, a volunteer paramedic back home, was overwhelmed by the townspeoples' generosity. "We were never strangers here," she said later. "Whenever we needed help someone was there. Everyone opened their hearts and homes to us."

The people of Matamoros also opened their hearts to the distraught American family, offering words of encouragement as the Kilroys searched the city from one end to the other. Often when they were in Matamoros, strangers approached them to say that they were praying for Mark's safe return.

Young Mexicans helped distribute Mark's missing posters. Some of the volunteers, like Mark, were college students. A few of them attended classes across the border at Texas Southmost College in Brownsville.

The Kilroys weren't forgotten at home, either. Santa Fe is a typical small American town, boasting a single main street and only one high school, but people there tend to look out and care for one another. Friends and even total strangers rallied behind the stricken family, offering emotional and material support. Auctions and garage sales were held to help finance the search. Thousands of inflated balloons were released carrying Mark's description and printed messages about his disappearance. And a yellow ribbon ceremony was also scheduled to demonstrate the town's hope that Mark would be found alive and well.

One of the many people to contact the Kilroys and offer help was Denise Sikes of Galveston County. She knew what the Kilroys were going through because her stepdaughter, Shelley Sike, a nineteen-year-old Galveston waitress, disappeared on May 25, 1986, as she was coming home from work. Police found the girl's car, but Shelley had simply vanished, and her family kept her disappearance in the public eye through a coordinated effort that included billboards and thousands of fliers. Two men were later convicted of her kidnapping, but her body was never recovered.

The family of Rene Richerson, another missing Galveston County girl, also used fliers and public appeals to keep up the search for their daughter. The twenty-two-year-old student at Texas A&M University in Galveston, disappeared October 7, 1988, and police reports state that she was apparently kidnapped from her job at a beach-front condominium office. No sign of Rene has been found, and the search for her continues.

While the Kilroys spent their time in Brownsville and Matamoros, Mark's friends at home and at school remembered him fondly.

Although Mark enjoyed a party as much as the next guy, he had a reputation for always putting his studies first. Often he studied so intently that he was bone tired when he finally closed his textbooks, and too worn out for the college beer bashes and fraternity activities.

Mark put so much effort into his studies because he always insisted on getting the best possible performance from himself. His friends respected him as being very intelligent. Some described him as "a super smart guy." In high school he consistently won math and science awards. He was a determined, confident student who excelled in his studies, and welcomed academic challenge.

The Kilroys were a well-to-do family with the financial and intellectual resources to mount an all-out search for their missing son. Mark's father, Jim, was a chemical engineer. His mother, Helen, was a volunteer paramedic. They quietly pressured the police into action, and quickly set up a well-planned manhunt designed to find their boy.

Across the border in Matamoros, Isidoro and Ericada Garcia faced a similar tragedy. They reported their fourteen-year-old son, Jose Luis Garcia

Luna, missing on February 25, 1989, after he failed to return home from his job at the nearby Villa Hermosa, where he worked tending cows.

It was there, however, that the similarities between the two families ended. The Garcias were farmers, far from destitute but completely lacking the financial or human resources necessary to publicize the fact that their son was missing under mysterious circumstances. There were no posters with little Jose's face on them, no posses scouring the area to interview potential witnesses, and no television shows to fuel public interest by illustrating how the boy may have been kidnapped.

In fact, publicity regarding Jose Luis Garcia Luna's disappearance was next to non-existent. Local police spent little time looking for the boy, because youngsters like Jose run away and disappear all the time. Reports were filed and a cursory search for Jose was made, but his disappearance was quickly forgotten by Mexican authorities. It was not, however, forgotten by the youngster's grieving parents, who missed him as much as James and Helen Kilroy missed their son Mark. In both cases, hearts would remain heavy until the answer was known.

Meanwhile, American and Mexican authorities strengthened their attempts to find Mark Kilroy. The college student's case had become the focus of a major manhunt on both sides of the border, and all stops were being pulled out in an attempt to find witnesses and uncover information that might shed some light on his bizarre disappearance.

As clues became more and more scarce, Bill Huddleston, Mark's close friend and the last person to see him in Matamoros, was placed under hypnosis by U.S. Customs Service agents. Perhaps, they reasoned, probing his subconscious might reveal information missed by more conventional investigative efforts.

During the session, Bill told investigators that he could see the mysterious Mexican man who had called to Mark. Speaking slowly, Bill recalled that the stranger had a circular scar or cut on his cheek. And Bill remembered that he called specifically to Mark as they stood near Garcia's restaurant. Bill said that he saw Mark stop to speak to the stranger, but that was all he could recall.

It wasn't much, investigators admitted, but it was something — a Mexican with a circular cut or scar on his cheek. At that point in the search, even a seemingly minor clue such as this might yet be developed into an important lead.

American and Mexican law enforcement authorities quickly began following up on the new information. Mug shots were pulled again from police files. Photos and printed descriptions of armed robbers, sex-offenders, kidnappers, and drug dealers were studied for evidence of a scarred cheek.

Known associates of the men in the photos were also checked out for the telltale scar, with no success.

Police were becoming increasingly desperate in their efforts to find Mark Kilroy and put a quick end to the whole sordid mess. Matamoros and Brownsville were sister cities, and bad publicity on either side could only harm the burgeoning tourist industry that fed them both.

But Brownsville and Matamoros shared more than an affinity for tourist dollars. Despite the fact that they were located in two different countries, for all intents and purposes they were a single city divided by the Rio Grande river.

Citizens from both nations walked or drove the four traffic lanes back and forth across the Gateway International Bridge every day for business, fun or education. Brownsville was the home of Texas Southmost College, attended by students from both the United States and Mexico.

Federal police in Matamoros were especially anxious to find Mark Kilroy because of recurring rumors of drug-related cult kidnappings throughout the area. Although unsubstantiated at the time, the stories surfaced with frightening regularity. Most police officials felt the stories were just rumors, but the thought of such kidnappings was unsettling.

There is much about Texas's Lower Rio Grande Valley, and the Mexican cities and towns just across the border, that is mystic and magical. Promoters pointing to the incredible harvest of fruit and vegetables from the fertile irrigated soil often describe it as "the Magic Valley."

But among Mexicans, and increasingly among many long-time Anglo residents, there is a strong belief in witchcraft, hexes, the Evil Eye and the work of *curanderos*, or shamans. Unlike the witchcraft of western Europe, which developed as a generally benign nature worshipping belief, the witchcraft of Mexico and the Mexican-American border areas is more likely to be malevolent. Witches are said to be able to fly, change shape, and to have mastered the secrets of invisibility so that they can more easily spy and cast harmful spells on the innocent.

Many Mexicans and Mexican-Americans from the Lower Rio Grande Valley, who attend Catholic mass by day, go to *curanderos* by night for healing of disease or fright illness — *empacho* — and, if they have enemies, cast hexes and evil spells. The supernatural is as common to the border towns as drug smuggling, violence and gum chewing Mexican child peddlers known as "Chiclet Kids."

Some Mexican federal police suspected that Mark Kilroy may have become the victim of border occultism gone bad and that he had been kidnapped by a cult. The possibility was not something they were anxious to publicize, especially in the absence of any hard evidence. But there were troubling indications that something strange was going on.

In October 1988, for example, a group of young children reported seeing some adults bury a body in a clearing near an orchard on Ejido Santa Librada, a collective farm on the parched outskirts of Matamoros. However, their tale was initially ignored by the adults it was told to and police would hear nothing about it until much later.

And in Texas, lawmen reported growing evidence of a bizarre marriage between drug smugglers and satanic cultists, each feeding on the other. The unholy alliance apparently is flourishing, law enforcement officers and cult experts learned, because many drug smugglers believe that black magic will protect them from the police and rival gangs.

The talk of cults, blood thirsty drug smuggling gangs run by ruthless *pistoleros*, and Mark's troubling disappearance took a heavy toll on the reputation and economy of the Brownsville-Matamoros area. Street posters printed with Mark's photograph were constant reminders that the American had vanished in the Mexican city without a trace, and it made other tourists nervous. And despite Cisneros's hopeful words and the reassurances of other public officials, tourism began to slump in the border region as wary *gringos* bypassed Matamoros and sister cities in favor of other vacation spots perceived to be safer and friendlier.

Matamoros's bars and restaurants were hard hit. The usually ear-splitting blasts of loud music from jukeboxes and bands was muted. Bar stools stood empty, and dance floors quiet. Idle waiters in restaurants talked with each other and glanced wistfully at empty tables that should have been crowded with tourists.

Most of the handful of North Americans who still dared to venture into Matamoros to sample the bars and shopping delights of the Avenida Alvaro Obregon traveled in groups, and fewer were willing to visit out-of-the way tourist bars or stay out late at night. They nervously admitted that the college student's distressing disappearance made them more cautious.

But the Mexican government on both the federal and local level was attempting to repair its tarnished image and restore the confidence of tourists to safely visit, vacation, and shop south of the Border.

Only a few weeks before Mark's disappearance the Matamoros Federal Judicial Police had recently received a thorough house-cleaning following the arrival of Juan Benitez Ayala. Young, determined and unafraid, Benitez was one of a new breed of Mexican lawmen, and he joined the Matamoros district FJP specifically as part of an inhouse cleanup of corrupt police officials. There were strong indications that officers with the Matamoros FJP and the Tamaulipas State Police were protecting the activities of drug smugglers in the area, and when Benitez's investigation was complete, FJP Commander Juan Manuel Ibarra and nine of his officers found themselves jailed for corruption. The smoking gun was the discovery in Ibarra's office of nearly five million in American currency believed to be payoffs from friendly drug smugglers.

Benitez was one of the few Mexican police officials who initially took a strong interest in finding Mark Kilroy. He and his officers worked closely with Mexican and American law enforcement agencies in the search for the missing college student, and Benitez struggled to clear the miles of red tape that normally hinders an international manhunt.

Sadly, it would be a search without a happy ending.

Adolfo de Jesus Constanzo — *El Padrino*

CHAPTER 3

Brujo

THE BIZARRE EVENTS which led to Mark Kilroy's baffling disappearance developed five years earlier when he was still a student at Santa Fe High School.

In 1984 another young man, who was bright, charming, and ambitious, left his home near Miami, Florida, and moved to Mexico City to make his fortune. But aside from his youth and quick intelligence, Adolfo de Jesus Constanzo was about as unlike Kilroy as he could be.

The handsome, light-skinned, twenty-one-year-old with the neatly combed shock of reddish hair was the American-born son of teenage parents who fled Cuba after Fidel Castro's Communist revolution. He was born in Miami Beach on November 1, 1962, when his mother was fifteen. But Adolfo's parents were married less than a year before they divorced, and he and his mother moved with her family to Puerto Rico. A few months later she married a successful businessman in San Juan.

Adolfo's stepfather was a caring husband and parent, and in a short time the family was increased by two more boys and a girl. Adolfo seemed to thrive in San Juan. He learned to play tennis, excelled at his parochial school classes, and served as an altar boy at the Roman Catholic Church he attended. He loved the candles, the robes, the arcane Latin phrases of the priests, and the esoteric ritual of the Church.

Unlike many of his boyhood playmates however, he was fastidious about his personal appearance and his surroundings. He wasn't even old enough to go to school when he began insisting that a robe always be left beside his bed so that he could put it on whenever he got up. When he was through playing with his toys, he put them away. And as he got older he was equally meticulous about arranging his clothes and other belongings in his room so that they were neat and properly stored. He insisted that his clothes be freshly laundered and neatly ironed, and fussed when they were not.

Although he got along reasonably well with other children, he avoided most of the rough and tumble play of other little boys. He didn't like to get dirty, and after a day of play in the hot sun of the island, he would usually return home as clean and with his clothing as neat as when he left in the morning. He was a Mama's Boy, and clearly preferred her company to that of anyone else. But he also spent hours alone, quietly absorbed in his own private pursuits. When he was ten, however, dark clouds began to threaten the boy's idyllic existence. His stepfather was diagnosed as having cancer, and the family returned to Florida to seek specialized medical care. He died a few months later, in 1973.

Adolfo's mother soon married again, and although he was adopted by his new stepfather, the boy and the man didn't get along well. Adolfo was jealous of the newcomer. And when the new stepfather attempted to discipline him, it sparked ugly quarrels with the boy's mother. Eventually the couple divorced, leaving Adolfo firmly in control as the man of the house.

He took his role seriously, and was attentive to his siblings. He was a loving big brother. Years later, his younger half-brother, Fausto Rodriguez would fondly recall the time when he was about thirteen or fourteen-years-old sitting outside the house and feeling sorry for himself because it was New Year's Eve and he was home alone. Then he saw Adolfo walking down the street toward him. Adolfo had been at a party, but knew his brother was home alone, and returned so they could spend the evening together.

Adolfo spent his teenage years in Hialeah, a palm-lined city of about 100,000 nestled along the northwest edge of Miami and instantly familiar to horse players for it's famous race track. Like many first generation Americans of Latin descent, Adolfo was fluent in both Spanish and English.

But where other young Latins in the U.S. with Cuban, Mexican, South or Central American roots, went on to develop skills in such areas as mechanics, computers, sales or law, Constanzo turned to darker, more sinister pursuits. From early childhood, his priorities were different.

His mother, Delia Gonzalez del Valle de Posada was a strong-minded woman who quarrelled with her neighbors. And some of them, at least, regarded her as a witch, or sorceress who conducted rituals of *Santeria*, an Afro-Cuban voodoo-like cult that employs the blood sacrifice of animals.

Mrs. Gonzalez del Valle would later insist that the family practiced only Roman Catholicism and deny that she was a *Santera*, or female practitioner of the cult. They almost always kept goats and chickens, domestic animals favored for *Santeria* rituals, in their back yard, and more often than not, the yard was overgrown with weeds.

After the son of a neighbor, Carmen Reigada, quarrelled with Constanzo's mother, Mrs. Reigada found a headless chicken on her rear stoop. And myriad tales of headless chickens, goats or geese left at doorsteps, and candles set up on street corners circulated throughout the neighborhood.

Residents of the middle class suburban Miami neighborhood complained quietly among themselves that members of the family, which lived in the house from the late 1970s until they were forced to move out by a bank foreclosure in 1984, were frightening. No one was sorry to see them go.

A woman who bought the house after the foreclosure reported that she found the remains of an altar with candles, wax and fruit when she moved in. The alter and paraphernalia merely added confirmation to the previous dark suspicions of neighbors. It seemed like a house where the mystery-shrouded Afro-Cuban religion, *Santeria*, had been practiced.

Despite the reputed dedication of Constanzo's mother to *Santeria*, a religion that promises to provide advantages and good things in this life, as opposed to most Western religions which promise paradise in the next, trouble continued to plague her long after she left the house in Hialeah behind. Three years after the move, authorities responding to a tipoff about possible child abuse charged her with child neglect, neglect of the disabled and trespassing. A police officer who kicked down the door of a supposedly vacant apartment, found her living there with several children and twenty-seven animals amid disgusting squalor. The floors were smeared with blood, urine and feces, and inside a bedroom two children were on a bed that was soaked with urine and excrement. A police spokesman later reported that one of the children was apparently mentally disabled.

Adolfo, who was raised in easier times for the family, seems to have taken readily to the ritual and trappings of *Santeria*. And when he was about thirteen, he moved on to master the rituals of an even more secretive religion rooted in the primitive beliefs of Africa, *Palo Mayombe*.

Consequently, when it seemed Adolfo, and his siblings were avoided by other neighborhood youngsters because their parents warned them not to play with them he didn't mind. He preferred to absorb himself in his own activities, and in the company of his own family. He didn't readily trust outsiders. But he did have a little circle of his own special friends.

He was still a teenager when he began frequenting homosexual hangouts in Miami and nearby Fort Lauderdale. His handsome square face, penetrating brown eyes, thick shock of red tinted hair and solid youthful body commanded immediate attention when he sauntered into the pickup bars. He had no difficulty attracting lovers for one-night stands, or longer romances of a month or more.

He was less successful as a student, and dropped out of high school when he was fourteen.

Early in 1980 he correctly prophesied that President Reagan would be shot, but survive, his mother later boasted.

But Adolfo's fourteenth year had more in store for him than discovery and confirmation of incredible psychic powers. It was also the year that he supposedly got a thirteen-year-old girlfriend pregnant, leading to the temporary interruption of his formal education after completing the ninth grade.

There was no marriage. The girl's mother refused to allow the couple to have any further contact, and adopted her newborn granddaughter as her own. The young mother and child quickly vanished from Adolfo's life.

He worked spasmodically at odd jobs, including hard manual labor pouring concrete for an uncle. The hard work may have helped convince him that life would likely be easier with a better education, so he took a high school equivalency test and was awarded a diploma. By 1980 he was attending classes at the Miami-Dade Community College studying psychology. He was still a fitful scholar however, and other troubles also intruded to interfere with his studies. He was arrested twice for shoplifting during his years as a college student, once for attempting to steal a chain saw from a Miami store in March 1981. Shortly after his second arrest he dropped out of classes. He was ready for bigger and more promising pursuits that would lure him deep into a menacing underworld of fabulous fortune, drugs, blood cults, and violent death.

When the handsome Adolfo wasn't making the rounds of gay bars in South Florida, he could often be seen in the *botanicas* of a Miami neighborhood known as Little Havana, because of it's heavy population of immigrant Cubans and their descendants. *Botanicas* are tiny shops that carry candles, herbs, figurines of the Catholic saints that double as *Santeria* gods, and other merchandise purchased for use in worship and casting of spells.

The enigmatic young man was a steady customer in the *botanicas*. He confided that he knew powerful spells that enabled him to summon spirits from the air and make them do his bidding. He boasted that he could attract riches, or bring down terrible curses on enemies. And he demonstrated his ability to cure illnesses merely by passing a live chicken over the body of a patient with his hands, muttering a brief incantation, then sacrificing the animal to the gods.

Adolfo was paid for his spells, and he was living well. But he had also attracted the attention of the police. They already suspected that it wasn't dutiful spirits financing his free and easy lifestyle. They suspected, instead, that he had moved from shoplifting to drug dealing. Adolfo was a high stepping, high-roller who dressed in furs and tailor-made suits, wore gold chains, and drove luxury cars to and from the gay bars he frequented. He had no job or salary, and it seemed doubtful that he could attract enough business from the spells to account for his curious wealth. But drug dealers in South Florida are about as common as maggots on spoiled fruit and if Constanzo was kept under any surveillance at all, it was a loose and fitful effort. There were thousands of known drug smugglers and dealers to watch.

Drug smuggling and dealing was so endemic in fact, that local, state and federal law enforcement authorities were joining in a massive crackdown aimed at shutting off the flow of cocaine, heroin, marijuana and other illegal substances into the state. Interdicting the massive flow of illegal narcotics through Florida's ports, beaches, rivers, canals and airports was an almost impossible job. Tons of drugs arrive daily on ships, boats and airplanes, their transport arranged by powerful crime cartels that have formed throughout the hemisphere.

Although tons of narcotics continued to find their way through the law enforcement net, the stepped up government efforts had put considerable pressure on the smugglers. By 1984, more smugglers were getting caught than in previous years, more drugs were being confiscated, and more dealers were being identified and removed from the streets. Some smugglers and dealers began looking for other, safer locals to operate in.

Adolfo, armed with his fluency in Spanish, and a hunger for power and riches, decided to move to Mexico City — the biggest, most heavily populated urban center in the world.

The Mexican megalopolis dwarfs Miami. More than twenty-million people are jammed into the city that Mexicans refer to as *La Capital*. Another 2,500 arrive every day, either by the painful process of birth or the equally agonizing act of migration from the impoverished and sun-baked countryside. By the end of the century, social scientists and urban specialists predict Mexico City will have swelled to a staggering thirty-million inhabitants, four times the number of people now living in New York City.

But Mexico City already has more human beings than it can handle. Spread out in a thirsty, sun-cooked valley, it is being suffocated by it's own population. A persistent, caustic blanket of dirty yellow and purple smog clings to the city, a foul mixture of fumes from motor vehicle exhausts, factories, and drying human and animal excrement trapped by high mountains that surround the capital in every direction. On the rare occasions when the smog lifts, the snow-capped volcanic tips of Popocatepetl and Iztaccihuatle can be seen dipping into the sparkling clear blue of the sky.

But the ready supply of food and water available in the valley is no more adequate than the supply of fresh air for supporting the burgeoning crush of humanity. Water is pumped into Mexico City from lower lying areas far distant from the metropolis, then pumped out again as foul smelling sewage and chemical waste. A constant column of trucks chugs into the city daily like a determined army of ants, carrying rice, beans, corn, fresh vegetables, fruits, eggs, poultry, fish and meat to the wholesale marketplace, *La Merced*.

The people of the city live in skyscrapers, red-tiled roofed homes of colonial Spanish style private homes, and in the miserable dirt-floored cardboard, wood, cinderblock, tar paper and corrugated tin shacks of the disease and crime infested *barrios*. Public school children attend the overcrowded classrooms in shifts.

But the young man from sun-kissed Miami was no poor *Indio* from Mexico's heat-blistered countryside who would consider himself lucky to find a cardboard and tar paper hovel to huddle in at night. And he had completed all the formal schooling he wanted. His cunning Machiavellian mind had other lessons to learn and to teach.

Despite his youth and his seeming lack of income, Constanzo settled into a comfortable apartment in an upper middle-class neighborhood a short distance from the *Zocalo*, the *Plaza de la Constitucion*. Located atop the ruins of some of the ancient Aztecs' most splendid architectural monuments, including their largest pyramid, during the daylight hours the *Zocalo* is constantly filled with cars and people, drawn to the twin-towered Cathedral, the shops and arcades, and the Presidential Palace with it's revolutionary murals by Mexico's most revered painter, Diego Rivera.

Constanzo often visited the *Zocalo*, but he wasn't in Mexico City as a tourist. Photos of the handsome, self-assured young man, dressed in the latest designer clothes and lounging casually near some of Mexico's most famous national monuments, were soon appearing in popular slick magazines throughout the country.

There was time during lapses in the busy work schedule of the personable bisexual, however, to ferret out some of the busier gay bars in the bustling capital city. He bought his high fashion clothing from expensive boutiques in the *Zona Rosa*, or Pink Zone, where only tourists and Mexico City's wealthiest citizens shop. And he met and romanced a pretty young Mexican woman, soon fathering his second child, a boy born in 1985 and named Adolfo. This time the mother was older. She kept her child, and although she and Constanzo did not remain lovers, she also continued to maintain contact with him. But Constanzo had other interests and considerations that overrode any feelings of responsibility he may have felt about his role as a father.

Almost as soon as he settled into his new surroundings, he began capitalizing on his proclaimed knowledge of spells and rituals designed to attract the attention of spirits and gods, and his ability to sell himself. He quickly became known as a powerful sorcerer who was as adept at performing *limpias*, ritualistic cleansings of the body to heal and protect, as he was at clairvoyant readings and prophecy.

In one of the most popular forms of the cleansing, which is part of Mexican *brujeria* — the generally benign form of witchcraft that is a meld of old Indian religions and Spanish Catholicism — he would pass an egg over the body of a client who believed himself to be under an evil spell. Then the egg would be cracked and the contents spilled into a glass of water, where the patterns could be read to determine the source of evil.

But Constanzo was not a benevolent *curandero*, the devoted mystic healers who treated the ill and removed spells for a few pesos and the gratitude of the afflicted. He was expensive, and ruthlessly brusque with those who couldn't afford him.

One Mexico City homemaker who sought Constanzo's help in a frightening five-minute confrontation after she and her husband were cheated out of a taxicab that provided their only income, was told by a young woman friend about a skilled sorcerer who could sort out her troubles. The younger woman knew Omar Orea Ochoa, a college journalism student with a high voice, and bright, pixie face, who was one of the sorcerer's male lovers. And with their introduction taken care of by Orea, the two women went to Constanzo's downtown apartment. The older woman and her husband were broke, and she was desperate. As the devoutly religious housewife inched timidly into the luxurious apartment, she was shocked by the *Brujo*'s greeting.

"Welcome to the house of the devil," he whispered.

Constanzo agreed that he could help the couple, but explained that it would be at the cost of her relationship with her Christian god. Constanzo advised that he dealt with other supernatural forces and those spirits and gods would become her new protectors. Then he told the stunned woman that she would have to pay thousands of pesos, amounting to more than $500 in American money, for a spell.

She stammered that she first had to talk over the plan with her husband, and hurried from the apartment. Once she was outside, she crossed herself and muttered a rapid and fervent prayer for protection. She never returned to the *brujo* — the witchman who had so casually admitted he was consorting with the devil.

Others were less sensitive about the sinister reputation of the powers the *brujo* called on for favors, and they had no problem meeting the steep fees he demanded. As Constanzo's reputation spread, he attracted a glittering array of some of the most famous and powerful figures in Mexico. He rubbed shoulders with stars of the entertainment world, with high police officials, and crime lords.

Incredible as it may seem, one of Constanzo's clients was Florentino Ventura, a career law enforcement officer who headed Mexico's branch of Interpol, the world famous International Criminal Police Organization based in Paris. It was even said that for a time the respected international police official became one of the clairvoyant's most devoted followers and considered himself to be Constanzo's godson. Whatever transpired between Constanzo and Ventura, it failed to head off a tragic quarrel between the high-placed police official and his wife a few years later. Ventura shot his wife and another woman to death, then killed himself. But he was hardly missed by Constanzo.

Movie stars, musicians, politicians, civil servants, even a beautiful fashion model and a physician were becoming the confident young *brujo*'s associates and clients. The elite of Mexico City, and of Mexico itself, came to him asking when they should release a record, what movie to produce, and the best time to settle legal matters or property transactions.

One time when a client asked him about selling a piece of real estate in Mexico City, Constanzo counseled him to hold on to it for awhile, according to the clairvoyant's mother, years later. She said her son told the man that a great tragedy would occur soon in Mexico. On September 19, 1985, the most devastating earthquake in Mexico City's history struck. Thousands of people were buried in the wreckage of their homes, offices, factory buildings and schools. Rescue teams rushed to the stricken city from all over the world, many of them bringing dogs to sniff out survivors.

More than 850 buildings were destroyed or badly damaged in the catastrophe, including homes of hundreds of lower middle income families in the Tlatelolco public housing project. Within a few terrible minutes, the destructive quake—measured at 8.1 on a Richter Scale of 10—had left some 70,000 people homeless. Constanzo's client sold the property he had been advised to hold onto for awhile, to the government, for a fat profit. New public housing was constructed on the land.

Constanzo's appreciative clients responded not only with money, but with all-expenses paid trips to such enchanting vacation spas as Acapulco and Guadalajara. Usually, he took young male lovers along with him. At other times he travelled alone and trolled for new conquests.

But not all the young clairvoyant's contacts in the glamorous world of Mexico's upper crust sought him out. Pop recording star and actor Oscar Athie was one of those whom Constanzo and his friends approached on their own, and the experience wasn't a happy one for the popular Mexican superstar. In fact it was eerily similar to that of Beachboy Dennis Wilson and Terry Melcher, the son of Hollywood actress Doris Day, experienced with the mad killer cult leader Charles Manson in the Los Angeles area twenty years earlier.

Manson was convinced that he was a talented guitarist and singer who should become a recording star and he was courting Wilson and Melcher — who was in the recording business. Manson planned to use them to help him cut a hit album and realize his dream. He and his clan were especially friendly with Wilson, but the cult leader turned on Melcher after he failed to show up to listen to Manson and some of his followers play.

Eventually, Manson went to Melcher's home looking for him. But the recording executive had moved, and the new occupants were movie director Roman Polanski and his actress wife, Sharon Tate. Consequently, the actress and several of her friends — not Melcher, who was said to be the original target of Manson's hate — died in the clan's grisly helter-skelter raid on the house at 10050 Cielo Drive.

If Wilson and Melcher were lucky to escape harm at the hands of a madman cult leader, Athie was equally fortunate. Constanzo and his followers also turned on the famous Mexican singer when he refused to go along with their plans for him.

Constanzo and his associates telephoned Athie in Mexico City and identified themselves as wealthy fans, who wished to hire him to perform at a concert in Miami. Athie is frequently approached by entrepreneurs to perform at concerts, and he was interested enough to meet with Constanzo in Miami, but after some discussion he rejected the proposed contract.

Constanzo wasn't satisfied to take no for an answer, and he and his followers continued their calls to Athie after the singer returned to Mexico, urging him to change his mind. The calls to the singer's home in Acapulco rapidly turned from imploring to threatening demands that he not only agree to perform at the concert but also pay Constanzo $2,000 to $3,000 for a good luck cleansing.

Finally, during one menacing call, Constanzo's friends warned that if Athie didn't change his mind and comply with the demands he would die slowly of a terrible disease.

Athie refused to back down. He continued to perform, but not for Constanzo. And he didn't become sick and die.

Age was beginning to take it's toll on Maria del Rocio Cuevas Guerra's career as a popular Mexico City fashion model, and her luck seemed to have gone sour when she turned to Constanzo for help. In fact, despite her glamorous career, she never believed that she had enjoyed the good luck she deserved.

· Constanzo said he could change all that with a ritual cleansing. As she bent from the waist, the handsome *brujo* chanted and traced some mysterious markings on her back. Then he lifted a small animal in his hands and passed the animal over her body, still chanting. At last he traced the markings on her with alcohol.

She required several treatments, but she followed his orders faithfully. And she dutifully handed over hundreds of dollars to meet his steep fee. But her luck seemed to change for the better, just as he had promised.

Not all of the baffling clairvoyant's clients were drawn from Mexico's entertainment and high fashion industries, law enforcement and government. Some of his most devoted and best paying clients were attracted from the nation's ugly criminal underbelly — thieves, pimps, prostitutes, and drug smugglers. They came to him for advice and protection.

For a steep price that reportedly topped out at $50,000, Constanzo offered cleansings and spells to protect drug smugglers from police and from

---

Brujo   27 other criminals planning hijacks or double-crosses of large narcotics or marijuana shipments. It was believed that his spells were so powerful that they would turn away bullets. Some whispered that the sorcerer had mastered the art of invisibility.

If some of Constanzo's claims of dominion over dark occult forces were hard for the more skeptical to believe, there was no question that he mastered the art of drug smuggling. While he counselled his clients, he listened carefully, and learned. As he insinuated himself increasingly into the confidence of the smugglers, he gradually moved into the trade himself. Soon he was travelling regularly between Mexico City, Miami, and the Matamoros-Brownsville border area, setting up drug deals..

He flew First Class, drove Lincoln continentals, gold Mercedes and sports cars, and wore diamond, sapphire, and ruby rings on every finger of both hands and gold necklaces around his neck. He purchased expensive jewelry and clothes for his lovers from the best stores, and twice in Brownsville he bought the same boyfriend $10,000 worth of elegant clothing in shopping sprees. He took them on trips to famous vacation resorts at Acapulco and Las Hadas. He wrote them poetry and love letters, filled with passionate promises of unending fidelity, then in a few months discarded them for new lovers. He was a social butterfly, and was always the dominant member in his romantic relationships just as he was in business matters. Even after breakups, his cast off lovers remained mesmerized by his charm and charisma. And gradually he put together a following of lovers, ex-lovers and other privileged middle or upper-class young men who were as personally devoted to him as they were to acquiring riches from the lucrative drug trade.

Although Constanzo could be generous to his romantic interests, he insisted that they respect his almost obsessive neatness, and even though he enjoyed play at famous resorts and spas he rarely smiled. And he never let down his guard when he was working on a drug deal. He was as stern and unforgiving in his personal life as he was in his business dealings. The *Brujo* didn't like to be crossed.

When a slender, dark-eyed transvestite stubbornly refused a demand to vacate an apartment Constanzo was renting in Mexico City, they quarrelled bitterly. Ramon Baez also used the name Edgar N. Baez. But when he proudly promenaded through the *Zona Rosa* in slinky cocktail dresses, high heels and hose wearing a long haired wig and makeup, he was known as Claudia Ivette.

He had slipped into the Claudia persona and was relaxing in his apartment when Constanzo and a companion arrived to tell him to get out. Claudia reacted hysterically, slamming doors, shrieking curses and shattering a vase. Neighbors, if they heard the noisy scrap at all, ignored it. And when the

Brujo stalked away from the apartment his face was flushed, but his eyes were bright, and his lips were turned up at the corners in a self-satisfied smirk.

Several days after the confrontation, the crudely dismembered pieces of a body were fished from the polluted waters of the Zumpango River just outside *La Capital*. Medical examiner's pathologists patiently pieced together the pasty gray chunks of softened flesh like a grisly jigsaw puzzle. The remains were those of a healthy, slender young man. He was identified through fingerprints and dental charts as Ramon Baez.

The waters around Mexico City, in fact, were becoming a favorite dumping ground for the grossly mutilated bodies of men and women who were apparently being ritualistically murdered. One after another, a series of bloated bodies, each weighted down with cement blocks tied with wire, were pulled from the warm water of lakes and rivers. Sometimes single bodies were recovered, at other times, two or three at a time. Two especially macabre elements of the mutilation linked the bodies to each other. The vertebra had been torn from the backs of each of the victims. And always, the hearts were ripped out, as if the victims had somehow strayed hundreds of years back in time to become grisly blood sacrifices in ancient Aztec rituals honoring the fierce Sun God, *Huitzilopoditli*.

But the glory days of the blood-thirsty Aztecs had ended centuries ago and Catholicism had replaced the ancient gods to become the dominant religion in Mexico. Blood sacrifice was no longer required to keep the sun moving across the heavens, the race healthy and strong, and to make the maize grow. And if baffled police even suspected ritual human sacrifice was linked to the mounting bodies they must have considered it an unlikely factor.

The violence that raged through the sprawling Mexican capital was more often tied to senseless domestic disputes, thievery and the thriving drug trade. And it was the drug trade that was increasingly drawing Constanzo from Mexico City to Brownsville and Matamoros.

Sara Maria Aldrete Villarreal

CHAPTER 4

A Border War

MATAMOROS HAS LITTLE of the urbane sophistication and worldliness of Mexico City, but it shares many of the contrasts.

With a population of roughly 185,000, it is the largest city in the state of Tamaulipas that runs along the Gulf of Mexico from Tampico north to the Rio Grande and the U.S. border.

Residents or visitors who can afford to eat in nice restaurants, can breakfast in the Cafe de Mexico in Matamoros, stroll in the *zocalo,* shop for blankets, serapes, and straw baskets at open air stalls, or in the well-stocked boutiques in the *Mercado Juarez,* dine on fresh game at the Drive-Inn, or sip salty margaritas and cool off with frosty bottles of Dos Equis in the Piedras Negras, Blanca White's or other comfortable bars while being serenaded with strolling mariachi bands.

Lusty young males can sample the fleshy delights of the local Boys Town, the seedy enclave of cantinas and whorehouses set aside from other areas of most Mexican border towns to accommodate the thriving prostitution trade.

And regardless of whether the shopping is done in the string of specialty shops offering clothing, pottery and jewelry that stretch along the Avenida Alvaro Obregon just south of the international bridge, at the *Centro Artesenai* — the government owned arts and crafts center, or in Boys Town, visitors can move in relative safety. If policemen are sometimes difficult to find in most areas of Matamoros, they can usually be located quickly and easily in the tourist areas. They are always no more than a scream or a bottle toss away in Boys Town where both local Mexican residents and party loving Texans who drive across the border in pickup trucks or dusty Blazers and Broncos provide a critical source of income. Preferably, the hell-raising Texans and the tourists pay in greenbacks for whatever goods and services they demand. Runaway inflation in Mexico can eat away large chunks of the peso overnight, and the comparatively stable American dollar is the currency of choice.

Prior to the Mexican War, Matamoros extended across the river into what is now part of Brownsville. That changed in 1846 when General Zachary Taylor planted the U.S. flag north of the Rio Grande, and constructed a fort. The fort was eventually named Fort Brown, for Major Jacob Brown, who died while defending it from Mexican attack.

During the American Civil War, both Matamoros and Brownsville became important outlets for shipping of Confederate cotton into the Gulf of Mexico and beyond. Matamoros continues today to be an important manufacturing and commercial center tied to the cotton industry. It also processes tons of sugarcane, operates tanneries and distilleries. And it is linked by air, railroad and highways to Monterrey and Mexico City.

But many of Matamoros's workers make daily crossings of the International Bridge to the Cameron County seat town of Brownsville, Texas. A bustling deep water port that boasts a large shrimp fleet and shipping, as well as canneries, petrochemicals, and healthy aircraft repair industry help support a population of 85,000 and make Brownsville the largest city in the heavily irrigated Lower Valley. It is the area's chief gateway to Mexico.

Not all the men and women who cross over from Mexico work in Brownsville. Many continue on through the towns, shopping centers and RV parks strung one after another in ragged file across the Lower Rio Grande Valley to orchards and fields where they pick the oranges and the area's famous pink grapefruit, cut the sugarcane or sorghum and provide the stooped backs and busy hands to harvest rotating crops of tomatoes, watermelon, canteloupe, cabbage, lettuce, and other fresh produce that grows in the rich, brown loam. Thanks to constant semi-tropical temperatures with hot days and warm nights that permit a year-long growing season, the Valley is one of the nation's most productive agricultural areas.

Many of the women who cross the international bridge from Matamoros work as domestics, handling the cooking, housecleaning, and childcare chores of busy Texas mothers with their own better-paying jobs outside the home. At night the Mexican workers walk or drive across the bridge, returning to Matamoros with their precious handful of American dollars.

Matamoros also has large areas where there are no dollars and few pesos, that mirror the grinding, hopeless poverty in the shantytowns of Mexico City. There are squalid, smelly slums where *Indios* newly arrived from Mexico's interior sometimes sleep in tents, cardboard boxes or simply stretch out in the open, until they can throw up or otherwise acquire a tar paper shack or one-room grey cinderblock house that fuse together among a crazy-quilt tumble of goats, chickens, pigs, and kids.

Children languidly play in the sun-dappled dirt or dust, poke through trash, and urinate and defecate in the streets or in fetid ditches scratched out of the earth to carry away human waste. And they gather at communal fountains, with buckets and tin cans to collect water for drinking and cooking.

The slums teem with children and provide many, although not all, of the

Chiclet Kids who hawk tiny squares of chewing gum to passersby near the bridge and in other areas of the city with all the aggressiveness of noisy crows. But most of all, Matamoros shares the corruption that has plagued Mexico City, and in the chronic despair of many of its less fortunate citizens.

The shattered backdrop of the slums is a perfect beacon and breeding ground for the poor and desperate who see the drug trade as a seductive avenue promising to lead them; from the lifetime of privation that has been their gloomy birthright. They are hungry to enlist as mules who transport marijuana and other drugs, as lower level soldiers, or fearless *pistoleros* in the violent drug and illegal alien smuggling wars that have crackled along Mexico's 1,960-mile border with the United States like an out-of-control forest fire. And the smuggling trade, whether for drugs, illegal aliens, guns, antiquities from Yucatan and Central America, or precious stones and metals, is a hungry demanding master that devours bodies and souls. Dead or injured soldiers are instantly replaceable.

In fiscal 1988 U.S. federal agents seized marijuana, cocaine and heroin worth $700 million, compared to seizures totalling less than $30 million five years earlier. The fabulous amounts of illegal money to be made have transformed the border towns into a war zone where powerful drug lords buy police and other public officials, families splinter into bloody feuding factions that kill each other off, and law enforcement authorities on both sides find themselves outnumbered and outgunned. U.S. Border Patrol agents are routinely outfitted with six-shot revolvers and bulletproof vests. Smugglers carry assault rifles with banana clips and laser sights for use at night, Israeli Uzis, and a bewildering array of handguns with 50 and 100 round magazines. When they are in a gun battle, they don't aim and fire. They spray.

In December 1988, a U.S. Customs sting operation led agents to a planeload of AK-47s, armor-piercing rockets, hand grenades and grenade launchers being smuggled across the border from Mexico by a drug trafficker.

At about the time that Mark Kilroy vanished from Matamoros, an agent attached to the Border Patrol Station at Brownsville, was in a van pursuing a suspected illegal alien near the Rio Grande. The suspect stopped suddenly, turned, dropped to one knee and squeezed off five shots in rapid order from an M-16 rifle. The border patrolman scrambled from the van, and escaped without injury. The incident was harrowing for the agent, but not unique among the helter-skelter savagery that rages along the border today.

The recent influx of refugees from Central America, especially El Salvador, Nicaragua and Guatamala, have made the situation even worse. Roving gangs of thieves and killers prey on both Mexican and Central American aliens who are led to border crossings by guides known as "Coyotes," or who try individually or in small groups to slip into the United States on their own.

The gangs, including avaricious Americans who have scented easy prey; rape, rob and murder with near impunity. The survivors, themselves involved in criminal acts by trying to enter the U.S. illegally, seldom complain to authorities.

Often the Coyotes purposely lead their charges into traps. Then after their victims are robbed, or murdered, the Coyotes return to Mexico for another group of desperate refugees.

The profitable drug trade has sparked even more violence than the traffic in refugees. But many of the smugglers deal in both drugs and refugees, sometimes in other goods as well. Violence is always lurking at the edges of the transactions, whatever the goods. The drug and smuggling trades are dependable, but demanding and unforgiving employers.

In Texas' Cameron county, which includes Brownsville, homicides nearly tripled in 1988 from the previous year. Violence has a trickle-down effect, and after a drug smuggler has machine gunned a competitor, it is easier to shoot a stranger over a parking dispute, to beat a spouse or girlfriend to death in a domestic quarrel, or to gun down a policeman after a traffic stop. In 1988, the last year for which statistics were available, twenty Texas policemen — including five in San Antonio — were murdered while on duty. It was the highest toll in sixteen-years.

There appears to be no limit to the devastating mayhem and violence sparked by the fortune to be made in the drug trade, and the contempt for human life is breathtaking. Cameron County Sheriff Alex Perez has seen the shocking results of the frenzy, and has talked about it with journalists. In one account the sheriff told of drug dealers armed with household laundry irons, who use them to sear away the flesh of informers or competitors. He talked of victims tortured terribly with blow torches, of bodies slashed open, and of screaming young men machine gunned and set afire in a car.

There are no rules of good conduct among the gangs. They murder rivals, betray confederates, and bribe police and public officials on both sides of the border with cold indifference. The huge amounts of money to be derived from smuggling has enabled them to reach some of the highest levels of law enforcement and government in Mexico. Official corruption blamed on drug money has become so accepted that some of the more powerful crime kingpins are sometimes described as 'narco-politicians.'

The wide-scale official corruption has been the uncomfortable source of bitter exchanges between authorities in Washington and Mexico City.

When Carlos Salinas de Gortari took office as Mexico's president on December 1, 1988, it was after his predecessor, former President Miguel de la Madrid, had suffered a staggering series of disappointments and public relations disasters.

De la Madrid, a handsome, hard-working attorney born in the state of

Colima on the Pacific Coast was a graduate of the Harvard Law School in the United States, and took office in 1982 after conducting an anti-corruption campaign. But during his six years in office hundreds of federal and local Mexico City police were cashiered for extortion and other crimes, the peso steadily declined in value, annual inflation rates cruised at more than 150 percent, unemployment zoomed, and real wages plummeted until the purchasing value of paychecks were cut in half.

De la Madrid's difficulty with Mexico's economic, political law enforcement, and narcotics control troubles inevitably spilled over into his relationship with the United States. He appeared to be unable — some American officials believed he was unwilling — to slow the flow of illegal aliens over the Mexico-U.S. border. And despite official and unofficial pressures from Washington, he seemed to be powerless to make a significant dent in the thriving trade smuggling drugs across the border between the two countries.

In a 1986 report, the U.S. State Department pinpointed Mexico as the "largest single country source" of marijuana and heroin moving into the United States. Some U.S. officials have estimated that as much as one-third of the refined cocaine smuggled into this country passes through Mexico. Mexican spokesmen insist that the amount of the drug smuggled across their borders is much less, about fifteen-percent.

U.S. law enforcement authorities and Washington legislators were especially incensed at Mexico's handling of the bold daylight kidnap and torture assassination of an American Drug Enforcement Administration, DEA, agent in Guadalajara in February 1986.

The bodies of Enrique Camarena Salazar and his Mexican pilot, Alfredo Zacvala Avelar were found in a shallow grave near the resort city after a month-long search. Almost two years later, early in 1988, the situation in Guadalajara was still so bad, that the DEA had to pull its agents out of the city for several days for their own safety.

Eventually, after many bitter exchanges between American government and law enforcement officials, drug kingpin Rafael Caro Quintero and five other men were sentenced on charges connected to the kidnap-killings. Although Quintero was given a thirty-four-year prison term on drug-related charges, he was never sentenced for homicide. Federal charges of conspiring to distribute cocaine were also kept open against him in Los Angeles.

Constanzo was a frequent visitor in Guadalajara. Mexico's second largest city was one of his favorite vacation spots. It was also the scene of a complicated, double-dealing drug scam, in which he and a confederate posed as U.S. narcotics agents to steal 4.4 pounds of cocaine from a dentist in the Western Mexican metropolis. Months later the man accused as Constanzo's accomplice, would be revealed to be a Federal Judicial Police Officer and a suspect with the Godfather in the Al Capone style slaughter of nine members of a Mexico City drug trafficking family.

Despite the disillusionment of many Mexicans and some American law enforcement and legislative critics with de la Madrid's administration, he left behind several significant economic achievements, notably a significant hike in the nation's economic reserve account that enabled Mexico to continue servicing its crippling $100 billion plus foreign debt, and his reputation for personal honesty. De la Madrid handpicked Salinas, his budget minister to be his successor. Like de la Madrid, Salinas was a Harvard graduate, but with a degree in economics instead of law.

Salinas rode to victory as head of the long-governing Institutional Revolutionary Party on a wave of tough rhetoric promising to attract increased private investment by controlling government spending to put the nation back on a stable economic path, initiate sorely needed new public works projects, clean up high-level corruption and declare war on the drug lords. He has done his best to make good on his promises, including his vow to clean up corruption and battle drug traders.

Mexico was barely four months into the Salinas administration when an elite squad of Federal judicial anti-narcotics agents swooped down on the hometown stronghold of suspected drug kingpin Miguel Angel Felix Gallardo at Culiacan in Northwest Mexico's Sinaloa state, and took the entire 600 man police force in custody for twenty-four hours. But Gallardo was in Guadalajara, where he was arrested hours later.

Although Gallardo was not charged with Camarena's murder, he was described by DEA Mexico City chief Ed Heath in a newspaper article as a major suspect.[1] And in another report, Alvarez described Gallardo as the "intellectual author" of the organization that executed Camarena. But some top law enforcement authorities in Mexico remained convinced that Gallardo had indeed, opposed the U.S. drug agent's kidnap-murder.

Gallardo, who was alleged to be the "Mexican Connection" with the notorious Columbian Medellin drug cartel which the DEA estimated was jointly responsible for pumping as much as four tons of cocaine every month into California, Arizona, and Texas, was charged along with six Mexican law enforcement agents, with a series of drug and bribery offenses.

In conjunction with the arrest, the raiding party also detained the entire 115-member police force of the Sinaloa capital city. Federal judicial police spokesmen later explained that they did not trust the Sinaloa officers and wanted to avoid a shootout.

Culiacan, with a population of roughly 360,000, marked up more than 6,500 murders between 1981 and 1986. Most of those killed were in drug

---

1. *Chicago Tribune*, April 16, 1989, by Storer H. Rowley.

wars by rampaging *pistoleros* wearing cowboy outfits, and riding in pickup trucks while shooting rival gangsters with machine guns. But unwary citizens also became victims by straying innocently into the gunfire. And young girls were sometimes snatched off the streets and raped. Before Gallardo's arrest and the Salinas crackdown, Culiacan was a city out of control.

Salinas came out of the starting gate with a vengeance, and the arrest of Gallardo and his accused police henchmen was only one of several dramatic moves against drug dealers, crooked cops and high-level officials suspected of corruption that the determined new president made in the first few months of his administration.

The chief of the oil workers union, one of the most powerful men in Mexico, was one of those arrested in the new president's cleanup campaign. And several of the nation's most successful stockbrokers were arrested on charges accusing them of a variety of violations.

One of his first moves in the rejuvenated narcotics war was to create a new office called the Permanent Campaign Against Narcotics Trafficking in Mexico, and to call for a 100 percent increase in anti-drug personal, and a $3 billion budget to finance the campaign. Javier Coello Trejo, a stern, uncompromising deputy attorney general who was highly respected among both U.S. and Mexican lawmen who nicknamed him, "The Iron Prosecutor," was put in charge of the new anti-drug campaign office, and determined young drug fighters were quickly assigned to areas known to have heavy drug dealing. Many veteran officers were retired, reduced in rank or shifted to other posts.

Everyone who travels any distance on Mexico's dusty roads and highways was made aware of the new president's determination to crack the whip on runaway drug dealing, when he ordered 3,000 soldiers and federal police to beef up 86 checkpoints at road blocks and border inspection stations around the country. The new stations were described by Mexican drug enforcement authorities as filters, to describe their purpose: to filter out cars and trucks headed for the U.S. border with drugs or other contraband.

Once stopped by sober-faced soldiers dressed in green uniforms and cradling automatic weapons, motorists were made to stand by their cars while black uniformed federal police probed the inside and undercarriage of the vehicles with flashlights and screwdrivers for contraband. Gasoline tanks were checked for double frames or bottoms. Trunks and doors were checked for hidden compartments. Grain trucks halted at the military roadblocks were checked by police with long poles. Bus passengers were made to exit and stand aside, while police checked through luggage and ice chests.

Drivers and passengers, both Mexican and American alike, were courteously asked where they were going and where they had been. Driver licenses and other identification were carefully checked. The policemen and soldiers sometimes collected bonus arrests of suspected criminals who had nothing to do with smuggling, but failed to squeeze through the checkpoints. Early in 1989 authorities picked up Mexican-born winery worker Ramon Salcido Bojorquez, when the bus he was riding to his hometown of Los Mochis, was stopped at a drug checkpoint in Northwest Mexico. Salcido was wanted in California as a suspect in the murder of his wife and two little girls, and the near-fatal throat slashing of a third daughter.

Police at the barricades gave special attention to vehicles coming long distances, or from cities like Jalisco and Vera Cruz, areas known for their crops of potent Mexican marijuana and for smuggling of more potent drugs such as brown Mexican heroin or cocaine from South America.

The Valle Hermoso checkpoint on the Reynosa Highway a few miles from Matamoros under the Matamoros Federal Judicial Police jurisdiction was one of those beefed up by the presidential order. It would eventually play a prominent role in the search for Mark Kilroy, as well as in the lives of Constanzo and his cronies.

In the meantime, however, the spirited drug control crackdown continued on both sides of the border.

In 1988 the United States also elected a new president, George Bush. And the former CIA chief who headed the nation's drug interdiction effort as Vice President under Ronald Reagan, appointed a tough, experienced, new anti-narcotics czar. William Bennett was named director of the federal Office of National Drug Control Policy, becoming President Bush's new point man charged with responsibility for formulating a new strategy for fighting the narcotics problem.

The U.S. was already waging a spirited battle against drug traffickers along the Florida coastline, the Mexican border and other trouble spots where drugs are ferried in by a steady convoy of aircraft, ships, boats, cars, trucks, and human mules. But some of the harried agents and authorities were disgusted by ugly suspicions that the U.S. was doing the job alone — or at least without the wholehearted assistance of Mexico, the Bahamas and other Carribean, South and Central American nations.

The DEA, Coast Guard, Border Patrol, Customs Service, even the Fish and Wildlife Service have found themselves on the front lines in the battle to interdict the tons of poison being smuggled across America's borders. And everything from drug sniffing dogs and informants to airplanes, state-of-the-art helicopters, sophisticated high-tech James Bond-type gadgetry, and radar screens manned with $18 million blips has been called into play.

The U.S. effort to cut down on smuggling of drugs and aliens across the border even led to construction of fences near El Paso, Texas, and San Diego, California, irreverently dubbed "The Tortilla Curtain," by INS agents. But the fences, seen as more of a defense against the crossing of illegal aliens than drug smugglers, were too easily torn down.

Some of the staggering costs of the anti-drug campaign has been reluctantly absorbed by the criminals themselves. The DEA began seizing an average of $2 million in assets, about forty-percent in cash, from the drug dealers every day.

In a desperate move to counteract the brutal firepower of the drug traffickers, the Drug Enforcement Administration, DEA, began arming its agents with machine guns and automatic rifles. The Border Patrol has added about 1,000 agents since 1986 to create a force of near 3,500. Agents practice with automatic weapons during courses provided at the Federal Law Enforcement Training Center in Glynco, Georgia. The training is critical.

Late in 1988 near Brownsville, a pair of Border Patrol agents shouted at two shadowy figures hugging the ground and lugging a large bag. The patrolmen identified themselves as immigration agents and ordered the suspects to stop. Instead they found themselves ducking a volley of automatic weapons fire. The agents fired back, and a few minutes later found one of the gunmen lying wounded near the Rio Grande. An automatic pistol and a forty-pound bag of marijuana were lying in the dust beside him.

Despite the stepped up drug interdiction effort on both sides of the border however, cooperation in investigative activities between the two countries and between various agencies was spotty at best — at worst, non-existent. Normal interagency rivalries were responsible for some of the lapses, and traditional American distrust of corrupt Mexican police on all levels accounted for more. Many American law enforcement officers were frank about their fears that any confidential information supplied to Mexican police or government authorities might wind up in the hands of criminals. There was plenty of justification for the distrust.

As recently as September 1988, armed federal district police stormed the Mexico City headquarters of the judicial police and freed two of their fellow officers who had been picked up on charges of assault and robbery. The incident was not something likely to inspire trust among Mexico's citizens.

But in February 1989, barely two months after President Salinas assumed office an elite team of federal officers and soldiers stormed the Matamoros Federal Judicial Police headquarters and arrested ten officers, including the station commander, Guillermo Perez Rodriguez, and the assistant commander, Juan Manuel Ibarra, while confiscating $5.5 million in cash and stolen jewelry. The officers were flown under arrest to Mexico City to face charges. Juan Benitez Ayala, an aggressive young officer with intelligent dark eyes, a shock of jet black hair, and a rare reputation for personal honesty, was named new commander of the Matamoros district.

One of the people that Benitez began keeping a close eye on in Matamoros was Adolfo de Jesus Constanzo.

Constanzo had become a frequent visitor to Matamoros and Brownsville, flying to the border cities at least once-a-month, often more frequently, from Mexico City. Sometimes he travelled with Omar Francesco Orea Ochoa, a saucer-eyed former journalism student he had met while prowling the gay bars of Mexico City's *Zona Rosa*. At other times he travelled with Martin Quintana Rodriquez, another almost pretty young man with a near constant look of petulance, whom he met while trolling the same haunts.

The U.S. Border Patrol was also watching Constanzo. McAllen sector Border Patrol Chief Agent Silvestre Reyes had information that the Cuban-American was smuggling aliens into Texas. The aliens were not all Mexicans. Matamoros, and other Mexican border cities, is alive with Nicaraguans, and other Central and South Americans, working as dishwashers, waiters, or farm help while waiting for money from relatives at home or merely biding their time until it is their turn to chance a crossing of the Rio Grande into the Promised Land to the north.

The Border Patrol's informants had indicated that Constanzo's gang was slipping a dozen, and sometimes as many as twenty, illegal aliens across the border at a time. The Patrol was attempting to infiltrate the gang with their informants. The information about Constanzo's suspected alien smuggling activities was not shared with Mexican authorities.

The *Brujo* was stepping up his business in Matamoros, and on one of his trips there he met Sara Maria Aldrete Villarreal as she was driving her father's car. He cut her off with his shiny new Mercedes on a bright, sunny Sunday afternoon and stopped her. He introduced himself, and told her that he was vacationing in Matamoros from his home in Miami.

The six-foot, one-inch, brown-haired Mexican beauty liked what she saw. Constanzo was not only handsome, but obviously had plenty of money. She was instantly taken by the worldly, smooth-talking stranger. Although she was twenty-four, her own world recently had been confined primarily to her family in Matamoros, and the campus of the Texas Southmost College in Brownsville where she commuted daily to classes as a physical education major.

Fixing her with his mystical brown eyes, Constanzo confided that he was a clairvoyant and offered to look into her future by giving her a reading with tarot cards. She accepted, and she was amazed at how much the cards told him about her. There were other readings, and a surprising number of the predictions he made as a result, turned out to be true. Then Constanzo took Sara to attend a secret religious ritual, unlike anything she had ever witnessed before.

The slender coed seemed easily drawn into his web, as much by her cur-

---

iosity about the mystical world of the supernatural that Constanzo claimed to have such command over, as by his sophisticated charm, hypnotic good looks and luxurious lifestyle. She considered him to be utterly fascinating and compelling. For a time, Constanzo seemed to be equally entranced with her. He telephoned his mother shortly after meeting Sara.

"Mama," he told her, "I met a girl born the same day as you." Mrs. Gonzalez and Sara share birthdays on September 6.

Sara quickly became Constanzo's lover. And she began living a bizarre double life.

In one existence she was the devoted daughter of Israel Villarreal, a Matamoros electrician, and his wife, Maria Teresa Aldrete; and an athletic and popular student at TSC. At school she was an attentive scholar, well-liked by her teachers and classmates, who became one of only thirty-three of the two-year college's 6,500 students who made TSC's Who's Who directory for 1987–1988. Students on the list are nominated by faculty, must have grade point averages of at least 3.0, and be active in campus organizations. She was president of the soccer Booster Club, which she helped organize, and won TSC's Outstanding Physical Education Award.

Few people, if anyone, at the school knew or cared that Sara was already living a sham and had accepted a scholarship to the school after falsely listing her residence as the home of a relative in Brownsville to qualify for resident alien status in the U.S. and a scholarship. It would be much later before her status as a top scholar would be questioned by critics who pointed out that her schedule was loaded with English, Spanish, and physical education courses — not the most difficult classes for a bilingual, athletic young woman. And it was hard to believe that such courses could provide the solid educational underpinnings that would be necessary to qualify her for medical school so that she could become the physician she said she had her heart set upon.

But the most serious crisis in her life occurred after a marriage on October 21, 1983, when Sara was nineteen, to thirty-year-old Miguel Angel Zacarias. The ceremony was performed in Brownsville by a Justice of the Peace, Alex Perez. The couple had the marriage license mailed to the same address in Brownsville that Sara later listed when she registered as a student at the college.

By 1987 the marriage had floundered. The couple separated, and late in 1988 were divorced. Sara moved back into her parents' neatly kept two-story grey concrete home in the same comfortable middle-class neighborhood near Matamoros's downtown shopping area they had moved into in 1970 when she was five-years-old. But after several years of marriage, Sara was ready to assert a new independence, and marked her return home by having an outside stairway built so that she would have privacy from her parents and younger sister while coming and going to her rooms on the second floor. She was popular, and neighbors regularly observed young men and women climbing the stairs to her apartment.

The urbane Constanzo, with his easy sophistication, vaunted supernatural skills, and Rasputin-like magnetism easily enticed the young divorcee and college coed into another world of romance, adventure, wealth, and power. She became his high priestess, as well as his lover, presiding with him and his coterie of followers at dark rituals in apartments, motel rooms, and rickety shacks in Brownsville and Matamoros.

CHAPTER 5

A Family Feud

SARA ALDRETE'S LOVE AFFAIR with the mysterious Cuban *Brujo* lasted for almost a month. Then Constanzo discontinued his sexual relationship with the special girl about which he had so proudly boasted to his mother.

Surprised at the abrupt break in the relationship, Sara asked her suddenly reluctant lover if he was married. He told her that there was no other woman involved. But it was true he had other lovers — They were men!

There was never really any serious question about the romance's longevity. As lovers, Constanzo preferred slender, well muscled, handsome young men like himself, who wore tinted sunglasses, designer jeans and expensive rings and bracelets.

Sara accepted his choice without any serious complaints. She not only tolerated Constanzo's various male lovers, but seemed to enjoy their friendship. And she soon had another boyfriend anyway. She began dating Elio Hernandez Rivera, a sturdy young member of a notorious Matamoros crime family.

Self-assured and ruthless when dealing with rivals within or outside his own drug-smuggling clan, Elio was smitten with the statuesque coed. In a love letter scratched out on a scrap of paper that ignored normal rules of punctuation, he wrote: "Sara I love you very much even if you don't believe it, I hope you save this as a memory of the one who loves you . . ."

She was pleased. She had an adoring boyfriend, and she was excited as well to have remained an important part of her former sweetheart's life. Just being around Adolfo was exciting. He had the air of the mystic, a sensuous image of magic and danger that was impossible to resist. And she was proud that she fulfilled a more important role for her former lover and his male admirers and followers, as the high priestess for the clandestine rituals they were increasingly participating in.

Despite Constanzo's personal homosexual preferences, both gods and goddesses were included in the curious pantheon of deities that he called upon in his rituals. And both the male and female elements were necessary parts of the hybrid magical mixture he believed to be necessary to work his spells. It was imperative that the cult have a priestess.

Sara was respected by Constanzo and his coterie of admirers, and she was rewarded generously for the role she assumed. She flew with Constanzo to Mexico City to shop in the Zona Rosa, dressed in expensive clothing, drove luxury cars, and wore jewelry with precious stones. When she was travelling with Constanzo, he introduced her to business associates and acquaintances who were not part of his inner circle, as his girlfriend, or his wife.

At TSC she showed off the latest fashions, and wore necklaces with curious metal medallions. She was cheerful and friendly, but she would change instantly and her voice and eyes would harden if anyone attempted to touch the medallions. She cautioned that something bad might happen to anyone who handled the necklaces, but coldly refused to discuss the strange symbols carved on them.

Sara always seemed to have plenty of money, and she spent it lavishly. Although she held down a work-study job at TSC's Physical Education Department that paid only $3.35-an-hour and was attending classes on a full financial aid grant of $855, she shopped in chic, trendy boutiques, travelled frequently, and casually paid $10,000 cash for her new Taurus. And she ran up enormous monthly bills on the cellular-telephone she carried in the car. Sara's grant at TSC was received under the U.S. government's financial aid program for college students, even though she was legally a resident alien and not an American citizen.

Despite her deep involvement in extracurricular activities at the college, she didn't develop close friendships with any of the other TSC coeds. There was no one special girl that she confided in about her studies, family or boyfriends. But there was at least one student she eventually came to share certain closely guarded secrets and confidences with. He was Serafin Hernandez Garcia, who was majoring in law enforcement.

Hernandez Garcia, who had lived in Houston and Mission, Texas, before moving with his family to Brownsville, was a privileged nineteen-year-old member of the same crime family as Elio. Although they were almost the same age, Elio was his uncle. Elio and the criminology student's father, Serafin Hernandez Rivera, were brothers.

Although at forty-four young Serafin's father was more than twice-as-old as twenty-one-year Elio, the brothers were locked in a bitter struggle for control of the family drug running business. The feud was developing into an increasingly relentless internecine quarrel that was ripping the reputed Hernandez drug family apart with an orgy of beatings, shootings, kidnappings, and murder.

The Hernandez gang was known by law enforcement authorities to operate one of the richest, toughest, and most recklessly ambitious drug smuggling operations in the Matamoros-Brownsville area — and the family appeared to be in the process of cannibalizing itself.

According to police investigators on both sides of the border, the pillars of the gang were the four sons of Elio Brigido Hernandez, a formerly poverty-stricken rancher from a small farming community a few miles west of Matamoros.

Saul Hernandez Rivera, the second eldest son, founded what was to become a drug-running empire in 1977 by smuggling marijuana across the Rio Grande from his father's modest spread, the Rancho Santa Elena. Initially the drugs were moved by the family into Texas, and eventually on into the U.S. Midwest. Saul began business by moving small amounts of the contraband, but he soon set up working agreements with larger suppliers in the area. He worked closely with Casimiro Espinoza, a local crime boss known by his nickname, "El Cacho." He also invested his profits and energy wisely, and quickly acquired marijuana fields in the Southern Mexico states of Yucatan and Oaxaca. Both are notorious for being among the four or five most productive states in Mexico for growing marijuana.

While Saul was in charge of a 250-acre marijuana plantation in Tuxtepec, Oaxaca, in 1986, it was raided by *federales* and tons of marijuana were burned. Benitez Ayala was the young FJP Commandate who led the raid.

One of the most spectacular outbursts of savagery in the gang war over control of drug smuggling in the Matamoros area occurred before Saul's slaying, when a team of *pistoleros* in a homemade armored truck slammed into a clinic where a gang boss known as "El Cacho" was being treated. Six innocent people were killed in the raid, ordered by the same rival gangleader who had put "El Cacho" in the clinic with gunshot wounds in the first place. "El Cacho" eventually died of his injuries.

With "El Cacho's" death, Saul moved up a step in Matamoros's gangland heirarchy and took over his fallen accomplice's operation. He set up a distribution network in Houston and, according to drug investigators, was believed to have appointed his older brother, Serafin Hernandez Rivera, to handle that part of the operation. Younger brothers Elio and Ovidio Hernandez Rivera were soon reputedly brought into the gang's operations, along with dozens of other relatives and cash-hungry smugglers on both sides of the border. Saul enlisted a ragged army of fearless desperadoes, young wild-eyed *pistoleros* — who were related only by their hunger for drug riches — into the crime family. One especially reckless recruit was a gunman named Alvaro de Leon Valdez. The twenty-two-year-old former peon was better known in the Matamoros bars and on the streets as "El Duby."

Marijuana began moving through the pipeline by the ton on a weekly schedule, and members of the once-poor Hernandez family started living the good life. They lived in nice homes, they had ranches and farms throughout

Mexico, drove big cars, partied with beautiful women, wore rings with glittering gems on each finger, dressed in flashy clothes and drank good whiskey. Their sons and daughters enrolled in colleges, and their wives burned candles and contributed impressive amounts of money to the local Catholic churches. They were on their way to becoming marijuana millionaires.

Saul was the heart and soul of the business — smart, tough, and absolutely ruthless. He had a vivid memory of the hard times his family experienced when he was growing up on the *Ejido Ramirez,* a communal farm just outside the village of San Fernando, about midway between Matamoros and Ciudad Victoria.

Saul had another advantage going for him: timing. He went into business in a big way just about the time early in the 1980s when the U.S. stepped up its war against drugs coming into the country through the Caribbean, which caused many smugglers to begin rerouting their shipments through Mexico, where there is a long, rambling border with the U.S., and innumerable peons and *pistoleros* who were desperate to earn a share of the illicit riches by smuggling drugs across the Rio Grande.

Although the Hernandez gang may have been considered small timers in the firestorm of drug smuggling that flashed along the border, Saul was determined that nothing would be allowed to threaten their success. The crime family was reputed to have the protection of a powerful Matamoros businessman. And shortly after the Matamoros newspaper, *El Popular,* named the family's alleged protector as the Godfather of organized crime in the border area, the publisher and a reporter who had worked on the story were murdered. They were shot down in broad daylight in front of the newspaper offices. Saul was the primary suspect. Authorities believed he either did the shooting himself, or directed it.

The ferocious gangleader had other problems as well. He had been wanted on federal warrants in the United States since 1984. That was the year he was arrested in Michigan with 20,000 pounds of marijuana, was released from custody on bail and fled across the border. It was too dangerous for him to cross back into the U.S. after that, so he directed the drug trafficking operation from Matamoros and depended on relatives to carry out his orders for distributing the contraband. There was never any question, however, that Saul was in charge of everything. He was the man at the top, he had the connections, the knowhow, and the final say in all important decisions.

Then in January 1987, just about six-months after the slaying of the *El Popular* journalists, Saul was gunned down in the street by *pistoleros.* The leader of the Hernandez gang was caught with his guard down outside the Piedras Negras, a popular Matamoros restaurant and bar. The thirty-eight-year-old gang leader and a former Mexico City policeman who was with him were riddled with machine-gun fire.

The ex-cop was Tomas Morlet, a twenty-two year Federal Judicial Police officer. Morlet had been arrested in February 1985 by fellow FJP agents in Baja, California. Following the arrest, police paraded Morlet in front of reporters from the U.S. and Mexico, and identified him as the mastermind of the murder in Guadalajara of DEA agent Camarena.

But the DEA didn't buy the story, and soon after Morlet's press appearance, he was released from custody. In May 1987, Mexican legal authorities indicted Rafael Caro Quintaro, former national commander of the FJP Armando Pavon Reyes, and several others for the slaying of Camarena.

Mid-day machine gun assaults on rival gangsters were not new to the mean streets of Matamoros, or to other Mexican towns that hugged the Rio Grande. The violence had arrived alongside the lively drug-smuggling commerce as it developed and spread along the border.

The Mexican border towns were under seige. Cold-blooded Columbian gangs had moved into the border drug wars, introducing cocaine into the scramble for illicit riches. Cocaine was even more profitable than marijuana, less bulky and easier to move. But the violence continued, and grew. There was no end to it. And Saul wasn't the only victim of the carnage.

Police agencies on both sides of the border were soon investigating doublecrosses, hijackings, robberies, and gangland hits carried out with incredible savagery.

Not all the violence was drug related, of course. The lucrative trade smuggling illegal immigrants across the border was also accompanied by unprecedented savagery, much of it directed at the aliens themselves. "Shootings, stabbings, murder, rape, sodomizing — you name it, we see it," a high-ranking Border Patrol agent said in a news interview.

In Brownsville, the Cameron County sheriff admittedly found the degree of brutality almost unbelievable. He told journalists of drug dealers who had used a laundry iron to slowly sear the skin from a shrieking captive.

Another man was tortured with a blow torch, which was used to cut his body up the spine.

And in yet another case cited in the sheriff's dreadful litany, three young men were machine gunned and their bodies incinerated when their car was set on fire.

Just when the Hernandez crime family needed most to stick together, it turned on itself. Instead of presenting a unified front to deal with the burgeoning dangers from desperate rivals in the drug smuggling wars, they began quarreling among themselves.

It may have seemed that as Saul's only older brother, Serafin Hernandez Rivera would be in line to take over the family business. But Elio, the youngest of the four brothers, had ambitions of his own. He planned to leap-frog both Serafin and the other remaining brother, twenty-seven-year-old Ovidio, to become the family's crime boss.

When members of the gang began choosing sides, there were some sur-prises. Serafin Senior's college student son, Serafin Hernandez Garcia, lined up with his uncle Elio. Ovidio also reportedly chose to stand by his brash and feisty younger brother. Several cousins, nephews, and a son-in-law supported the elder Serafin.

Serafin was having other troubles, in addition to the unpleasant sur-prises in the family's choosing of sides. Saul was in his grave barely four weeks before drug agents broke up a scheme to land a load of marijuana on an isolated airstrip near Bryan, Texas, northwest of Houston. At the last minute the airplane turned back to Mexico, without attempting to land. But drug agents picked up the senior Serafin as he was apparently waiting for the plane. Seven other people were arrested on drug charges as well.

The airplane pilot's sudden change of mind led to strong accusations a few months later by Texas Attorney General Mattox that someone in author-ity had tipped off the smugglers about a planned drug bust. And Mattox added that he was talking "about corruption on our side of the border."

Whatever may have prompted the pilot's actions, Serafin was never brought to trial on the charges. A prosecutor was later quoted in the press as saying authorities were hoping that he would lead police to others higher up the ladder in the drug trafficking network.

The arrest couldn't have been timed better for Elio and his ambitions of taking over the family business, even with Serafin free on bail. The mere fact that Serafin was free, tended to taint him, with some suspicion of possible collusion with police, by apprehensive drug runners. That and the charges hanging over his head were enough to severely hobble his effectiveness as a prospective leader.

There were no suspicions about Elio's reliability, or his loyalties. He had never been arrested, and his relative youth and plump appearing but decep-tively muscular body were misleading. Of the surviving brothers, he was most like Saul. He was tough, crafty, ruthless and ambitious. Nevertheless, when Saul died the family lost many of its most important contacts in the drug underworld. And other high ranking criminals were apparently taking a wait and see attitude toward reestablishing working relationships with the Hernandez family until they could determine the true leadership and staying power of the troubled gang.

The tensions and bad blood that was crippling the family unity became a matter of public record when Elio and the younger Serafin reported to the Brownsville Police Department that Ovidio and his two-year-old son had been kidnapped from the Amigoland Mall. The young men were in tears, and scared to death that the little boy would be hurt. Investigators determined that the abduction was apparently tied to the loss of $800,000 in a botched drug deal that set one faction of the family against the other. The key suspect in the affair was one of the kinsmen who was supporting the elder Serafin.

A few days after the kidnap however, police were advised that family members had settled the problem amicably among themselves and there was no need for further involvement by law enforcement agencies. Ovidio and the child were released unharmed, and police did not file charges against anyone in the complicated case. Ovidio didn't bother to go to police headquarters to reclaim his new 1988 Chevrolet pick-up truck, that had been left abandoned in the mall parking lot during the abduction, until eight months later, a few days before authorities began digging up bodies at the Santa Elena Ranch.

Elio realized that if the family was ever to hang onto its place in the drug running heirarchy of the border towns, they would have to end the destructive internecine quarrels. They would have to again join forces behind a strong leader with good workable contacts among more powerful elements in the drug underworld. And the leader would have to have the ability to protect them from police and rival gangs. If Elio was going to lead the gang he had to move fast before more damage was done by the quarrelling.

He was introduced to Adolfo de Jesus Constanzo.

Accounts of just how Elio actually met Constanzo differ. Some say that Sara was the conduit, that she introduced her old boyfriend, Adolfo, to her new sweetheart, Elio, after learning that they shared similar business interests. According to statements to the press by Commandante Benitez Ayala, Sara told Elio that she could arrange for him to meet a man who would protect him and make him a millionaire.

Other accounts credit "El Duby" with arranging the fateful meeting. Those versions indicate that the malevolent Matamoros gunsel had heard that Constanzo had valuable connections with powerful drug families in Central Mexico. "El Duby" had reportedly heard other stories, as well, that focused on Constanzo's strange mystic powers that enabled him to summon protection from the spirit world for gangs and individuals whose surreptitious activities could be expected to lead them into dangerous conflict with criminal rivals or police.

Regardless of who arranged the meeting, it has been established that Elio travelled to Mexico City to meet the vaunted *Brujo*. Some law enforcement authorities later came to believe that he ended up offering Constanzo half of the family's drug profits in return for sharing his contacts and providing protection for the family on both the material and supernatural planes of existence.

Constanzo knew people in the highest echelons of the Columbian and

Mexican drug underworld who could provide the raw product — marijuana and cocaine — to be moved across the border by the Hernandez family. He knew how to channel bribe money to the proper police and other government officials in Mexico for protection. He had the knowledge, connections and spunk to deal with stronger rival gangs who might try to move in on or doublecross the Matamoros hoodlums. And he had gods, devils, and the dead on his side.

During Holy Week, 1988, *El Padrino* first imbued Elio with his personal spirit protection.

CHAPTER 6

El Padrino

ADOLFO DE JESUS CONSTANZO was exactly what the Hernandez gang needed to make it a driving force once again in the region's drug trafficking world. He was wise in the ways of dealing with rival gangs, but he offered more than simple brute violence. He also brought members of the gang together with promises of supernatural protection — probably something no other gang could promise.

The occult aspect of Constanzo's promised protection served two purposes. It made gang members feel safer about their criminal activities, and it gave Constanzo an unspoken, yet powerful, means of control over the group.

The young man Mexicans called *El Cubano* (because of his Cuban extraction) was a charismatic leader who offered the Hernandez organization discipline and structure that it previously lacked. Under his unique leadership, the previously undisciplined clutter of border ruffians was molded into a family-like structure. Soon gang members were referring to Constanzo as *El Padrino* — the Godfather. It was an apt title. Constanzo ruled with an iron fist, promising members the world if they carried out his orders implicitly, but doling out brutal punishment for anyone who broke the rules he established. One of his strictest taboos forbade gang members from using the drugs they were smuggling across the border. Alcohol was permissible, but the use of cocaine — and except as part of religious rituals, marijuana — was not allowed. One gang member didn't listen, and snorted cocaine in the presence of *El Padrino* himself. Enraged at the flagrant act of disobedience and disrespect, Constanzo had the man killed on the spot. Needless to say, no one sampled the gang's drugs from that day on.

Constanzo made sure that everyone knew there would be plenty of money flowing in if gang members obeyed his command — but there was no room for unbelievers. Gang members were either in or out, he said. There was no middle ground.

Constanzo's followers were awed and intimidated by his reputed mystical powers. They were convinced he could sense disloyalty within the group, and would deal with it harshly and quickly. When two gang associates were suspected of being police informants, Constanzo ordered them bound and gagged. They were tortured mercilessly, then dismembered. The incident provided a dramatic lesson in loyalty and obedience.

The hard line worked. The Hernandez gang became the Constanzo gang, but no one complained. *El Padrino* was proving himself an able leader with a keen eye for business and management. He knew which policemen to bribe for optimum protection and who to sell drugs to for optimum profit. Before long the ruthless band was smuggling an astounding 2,000 pounds of marijuana — worth more than $200,000 — across the Mexico-U.S. border every week.

In Brownsville, the revitalized gang's successes were attracting unwanted attention. By late summer 1988, Lieutenant Gavito and other U.S. law enforcement officers were taking a close look at the Hernandez crime family. Gavito was doubtful about the integrity of some of the police in Matamoros, and suspicious that the Hernandez gang might be buying protection. In Matamoros, gang members were openly boasting they had the police there on the payroll.

Some of the American lawmen suspected that Constanzo, for all his canny boldness, ruthless intelligence, mysticism and panache, was answering to higher-ups — possibly Mexican, Colombian, Cuban, or other elements of the American crime syndicate.

But there was another price to pay for the incredible success of the gang. Constanzo introduced dark occult rituals, and advised his criminal clansmen that fearsome and jealous gods were responsible for the organization's rise to the top. The demonic deities protected gang members, he advised, by creating an *escudo magico de sangre,* a magical shield of blood that made cult members invisible to rival gangsters and law officers, prevented bullets from penetrating their bodies and made them immune from arrest. They could not be stopped, as long as they offered regular sacrifices to the blood-thirsty gods. "We believed," one gang member later recalled. "We were too scared not to believe."

Just as she had apparently helped arrange for Elio's initial meeting with Constanzo, Sara urged him to become more deeply involved in the black magic rituals. He was assured that his troubles would be solved as soon as he joined in. It was only a short time after that when Elio joined with Constanzo, Quintana, three other men and Sara, for a ritual that the Godfather promised would improve their fortune one-hundred-percent. Sara served as priestess at her married boyfriend's initiation. She became his Godmother.

As shifting patterns cast by the yellow light of the candles played over their taut faces in the gloom of the darkened shed, Constanzo softly blew marijuana smoke into their ears and poured a cheap alcoholic drink, *Agua ardiente,* onto their exposed necks. Quintana chanted unintelligible prayers, in a curious language, to end the bloodless ceremony. Experts much later would surmise that he was speaking Bantu, an old Congo tribal language. When the men left, they were told by Constanzo to bring live roosters and turtles with them when next summoned to the shack.

In the beginning, all the sacrificial victims were animals — goats, roosters, and turtles — whose death and blood were offered to appease the gang's primitive spirit protectors. Constanzo performed the dark rituals at a special sacrificial altar, while most other gang members waited outside. A few of his most favored lieutenants were sometimes allowed inside to assist in the rituals, but often even they were blindfolded with black scarves and could only listen to the eerie incantations muttered by *El Padrino,* and shiver at the death shrieks of the animals.

As Sara had done for him, Elio talked his nephew, Serafin, into joining the black magic rites. Almost immediately, Serafin's grades at TSC improved.

When Constanzo advised one day that the thirsty gods were demanding a human sacrifice, members of the clan agreed without question. No one dared cross *El Padrino.*

According to a later reconstruction by police and gang members of the cult's blood rites, the first person believed to have been sacrificed was a twenty-five-year-old man from the village of San Luis Potosi, who had been hitchhiking on the Reynosa Highway on his way to Rio Brava. He was picked up by gang members, and asked to be taken to the bus station in Matamoros. Instead, he was brought to the ranch hideaway and bound with masking tape.

Constanzo oversaw the sacrifice, enlisting the help of his bodyguard and lover, Quintana. Together they slashed the terrified victim's throat, then drained his blood into a large cauldron as prayers were chanted. The hitchhiker was buried on the ranch. He would be the first of many.

Human sacrifice provided the gang with even greater protection from police and rivals trying to move in on the organizations' lucrative operation, *El Padrino* explained. But the ceremonies also had a more subversive effect. They reinforced his power over his followers. After each ceremony, he was considered with renewed reverence; his followers ready to carry out his every command.

Primitive religious practices were becoming increasingly common in drug smuggling operations, especially among Cubans or Colombians. From 1985, when the Texas Department of Public Safety first began collecting the data, through 1989, investigators logged more than 225 cult-related crimes in the state. Most occurred during 1988, and most were tied to drugs. Afro-Caribbean religions are becoming the religion of the drug dealing underworld. One detective described it as being as much a part of the drug trade as the guns and the violence.

"We see more Cubans and Colombians infiltrating the drug trade, either working with old-line Mexican drug families or taking over. As they come in, they're bringing this supernatural stuff with them. What makes it scary is they're finding believers," a Texas-based DEA agent explained to reporters. In most cases, the agent added, the gangs are practicing Afro-Caribbean-based religions such as *Santeria* or *Palo Mayombe*.

Investigators believed Constanzo was merely motivated by greed. He loved money and all the expensive things it could buy. And the Hernandez smuggling gang was his key to riches.

Constanzo also understood the subtlies of group dynamics: how to bring people together and keep them in line. And murder — whether it was a revenge killing or ritual sacrifice — was one of his most efficient ploys. Once gang members killed, they were fully compromised and Constanzo literally held their destines in his hands.

One of Constanzo's most helpful enforcers was a small-time *pistolero* from Matamoros named Alvaro de Leon Valdez — also known as *El Duby*. Constanzo took *El Duby* under his wing, and he quickly became known as *El Padrina*'s "god son." *El Duby* had a hair-trigger temper that matched his trigger finger. And although he was only twenty-years-old when he first met the Godfather, he was already respected in Matamoros for his savagery and fearlessness.

His reputation as a killer was made on July 23, 1988, when he gunned down Lauro Martinez Massip, the twenty-year-old son of a well-known Matamoros businessman, and Gerardo Garcia, the twenty-two-year-old nephew of a former Matamoros mayoral candidate, in Los Someberos. Twenty-year-old Lisandro Martinez, Lauro's cousin, was wounded in the attack. Constanzo was reportedly seen in the popular tourist bar — which Mark Kilroy visited a few months later — the night of the double-murder. Police were unsure of any connection he may have had with the killing, however. And de Leon Valdez claimed he didn't meet Constanzo until after the shooting. He fled across the border to Texas, then returned to Mexico and hid out at the Santa Elena Ranch. It was there he said he was first introduced to Constanzo, and the Godfather asked if he wanted to earn some fast money.

El Duby was one of Constanzo's strongmen and became one of his most trusted bodyguards, but Sara Aldrete was the gang's *La Madrina* — its Godmother, Constanzo brought her into the cult and made her the organization's "witch."

Long after their ill-fated romance ended, Sara remained enthralled with Constanzo and his incredible wealth. He showered her with gifts. But the real reason Sara continued to follow him after the love affair ended was because he had an "enigmatic, mysterious, and interesting personality," she later told police. "Sara always liked it when he told her what was going to happen in the future," a Mexican prosecutor later observed.

Sara even got along well with the lovers, Orea Ochoa and Martin Quintana Rodriquez, who had apparently displaced her in the Godfather's affections. For a time the two men shared near equal roles as Constanzo's preferred lovers. Quintana played the role of the "husband," Orea Ochoa the "wife." But *El Padrino* was always the center of attention in the curious *ménage à trois*.

Sara had definitely changed. Her association with the Constanzo gang dramatically altered her personality. She had developed a dark side, though she struggled valiantly to keep it hidden.

When the shocking news of Sara's suspected criminal activities were made public months later, students gathered to compare notes about the quiet coed, and some strange stories began to surface. One story recounted the night Sara persuaded three college boys to watch the movie *The Believers* with her. Afterward, she stood up and began to preach about the occult and its attractions. While she may have been trying to bring them into the cult, the boys had been drinking heavily that night and simply believed she was trying to impress them by acting spooky.

Another account traced her friendship with three girls from the Mexican resort town of Tampico, on the southern tip of Tamaulipas State on the Gulf, who were on the volleyball team. Sara frequently treated them to dinner in fine restaurants, then drove them to the Sheraton Hotel for dancing. She paid for everything. And one time she advised them that if they ever needed anything, or wanted to get rid of someone, to let her know.

One classmate who often saw Sara at TSC noticed that the lanky, fair-skinned beauty always seemed to show up with a fresh injury almost every week. Sometimes she came to classes on crutches, or she would be wearing a neck brace. Sara never offered an explanation for the injuries. She appeared to have many secrets in her life that she wasn't prepared to share.

Much later, police speculated that one especially tawdry aspect of Sara's incredible life called for her to lure naive young men into the cult with promises of sexual favors. They also considered the possibility that Sara became a black widow of sorts and used the lure of sexual delights to draw unsuspecting males to their deaths as human sacrifices, or victims of drug-dealing double-crosses and revenge slayings.

During Sara's last semester at TSC, she tried to entice two members of the college baseball team to accompany her for a fun-filled weekend in Matamoros. She was an alluring head-turner, but the men, both blond-haired, blue-eyed Anglos, declined the invitation. Their reluctance may have saved their lives.

The fascination of Sara and Constanzo with the movie *The Believers* also played a major role in recruiting new members into the cult, as well as in bolstering the occult beliefs of those already a part of *El Padrino*'s crime family. The frightening videotape was repeatedly screened for the cultists, to help Constanzo reinforce the promise that human sacrifice could be used to acquire wealth and power.

The film stars Martin Sheen as a New York Police Department psychologist who stumbles upon an evil black magic cult that sacrifices children to the gods in return for unbelievable power. The psychologist becomes reluctantly involved in the cult, which bears a resemblance to the dark Afro-Caribbean religions *Santeria*, and the more ominous necrophilic *Palo Mayombe*, when his young son finds a small shell used in a blood ritual while walking through Central Park. The moment the boy touches the shell, he is magically chosen as a sacrificial victim.

The movie depicts the cult's magic as chillingly strong and capable of controlling, or even killing, anyone who stands in its way. It was a movie Constanzo cunningly used to brainwash his followers. It became a powerful tool of mind control.

Constanzo originally used an altered version of *Santeria* in his rituals, then swung sharply to the more twisted *Palo Mayombe* after watching *The Believers*. It is believed it was only after he first watched the movie that he began demanding human sacrifice.

Some experts in the occult now speculate that Constanzo was dedicated to a particular *Palo Mayombe* spirit force known as Oggun, the patron saint of criminals and criminal activity. Considering Constanzo's cult and drug-trafficking activities, the theory made sense. Such a pact between an evil man and a diabolical spirit could be seen by believers to explain how Constanzo managed his early success.

Constanzo was authoritarian and unforgiving, and he was incredibly charismatic. He gave structure to the disordered lives of his followers. He performed the difficult task of successfully merging his skillful effeminate Mexico City gay brigade, with the disorganized band of border ruffians whose ferocious quarrelling had been stealing their energy and draining their resources. At last, under *El Padrino*'s unforgiving tutelage, they had come to consider themselves part of the same cohesive clan of criminal kinsmen, a unified family of drug smugglers, killers and thieves. And Constanzo was their unquestioned leader. The supernatural element of ritual death only brought them closer together.

Blood and power rituals can easily sway the naive, confused and disillusioned. They can be made to believe the wildest claims of magnetic leaders. But the leaders themselves may be no more than enterprising cynics who use the belief systems to gain respect and maintain control. Whether or not Constanzo was a cynic, charlatan, or a true believer, his leadership worked.

Just as Sara reputedly used sex to maintain power over her fellow cult members, her mentor used religion tempered with a heavy dose of fear and violence. As time went on, he gained unremitting control of his sycophants with blood-curdling threats of torture and death, followed by hellish agony in the afterlife, if they dared question or disobey. His gods were powerful and they would exact agonizing vengeance on the body and soul of anyone foolish enough or unlucky enough to cross him, he cautioned his superstitious followers.

Wherever the Godfather moved, whatever element of society he found himself in, he was a master of his environment. His ego was bloated with power and success, and he quickly proved himself ruthlessly adept at the double-cross of other drug smugglers. He cajoled, seduced, lured, and cheated friends and enemies. Alliances lasted only as long as they were useful to him. If there was an underworld code of honor on the border, it was remorselessly disregarded by *El Padrino*. He boldly stole from his suppliers whenever he suspected that he could get away with it, frequently killing rivals in the process. When others tried to double-cross him, he ordered them butchered. His retribution was swift and sure. Their fate was terrible proof that the gang was to be feared and respected. And submerged in the firestorm of violence that accompanies the runaway drug smuggling along the border, the murdered men were hardly missed. Under *El Padrino*'s firm tutelage, the gang had become a methodical, efficient killing machine, stopping at nothing to further their drug trafficking interests.

But drugs weren't the only thing Constanzo and his pals were smuggling into the United States. Border Patrol agents strongly suspected that the Godfather was also involved in sneaking illegal Mexican aliens into the country. Constanzo was under investigation by American authorities for smuggling aliens across the Mexico-U.S. border several months before the heinous murders were uncovered in Matamoros.

"Constanzo was an alien smuggler," one sector Border Patrol Chief Agent told reporters. "We had him pegged as early as six months (before the slayings were discovered)."

Authorities believed Constanzo and his gang were smuggling perhaps twelve to twenty people across the border at each crossing. The murderous clan's ranch hideout and staging area was only a quarter-mile from the Rio Grande River, and the Border Patrol suspected there was a good chance he was using it to sneak desperate wetbacks into the United States.

The Border Patrol was trying to infiltrate the gang with informants when the serial killings and smuggling operation was uncovered. The illegal traffic in aliens suddenly paled in comparison to the crimes committed at the Hell Ranch.

As Constanzo worked to increase his powerbase and smuggling operations, police watched with mounting concern a rapidly burgeoning list of men and boys who were vanishing from the Matamoros area.

One of the missing men was Moises Castillo Vasquez, a fifty-three-year-old resident of Houston. He had vanished after advising his family that he was travelling across the border to tend the corn crop he had planted a few miles outside Matamoros. Months after the Houston man was last seen, his seventy-two-year-old father, Hidalgo Castillo, still searched for him.

The heart-broken Brownsville parent looked every where for his son, trudging wearily up and down dusty back roads, snooping around tiny ranches, and inspecting fields planted with new crops. But the old man overlooked the only real clue to Moises's whereabouts.

Children told the missing man's father that they had seen men burying someone in the orchard of a collective farm two miles south of the Santa Elena Ranch. The old man and other adults paid little attention to the story, passing it off as nothing more than youthful imagination. But as time passed, Hidalgo Castillo began to wonder if the children's fanciful story could be true — and if the person the strangers had buried was his son. But he wasn't yet ready to go to the reputed gravesite and dig. Not just yet. He was desperate to believe that his son, a hard-working husband and father of twelve children, was still alive.

Monica de Leon understood Hidalgo Castillo's dread. Her husband, thirty-nine-year-old Hector de la Fuente, had also been missing for several months. The couple lived on a small communal farm west of Matamoros; one day Hector simply didn't come home from work. The worried housewife notified authorities, but nothing came of their brief investigation.

Constanzo's confidence and arrogance was soaring. He seemed to be impervious to the law and rival gangs. His connections in the supernatural and material worlds appeared to be cloaking the gang in an impenetrable shield that protected them from all harm.

Then one of the Godfather's most trusted associates, twenty-two-year-old Elio Hernandez Rivera, made a mistake.

Examples of drug and cult paraphernalia found.

More examples

CHAPTER 7

The Vulnerability of Invisibility

A HANDFUL OF *FEDERALES* and soldiers were manning a drug interdiction roadblock on Highway 2 between Matamoros and Reynosa on a typical sweltering Sunday afternoon when a silver Chevrolet pickup truck roared past the barricades.

The driver kept his eyes on the road ahead, neither speeding up nor slowing down, seemingly oblivious to the consternation behind him as the startled officers frantically signalled for him to stop. Smartly dressed in crisp military uniforms, and heavily armed with a bristle of handguns and automatic weapons, the squad would have been intimidating to most any driver. Mexican police are notorious for itchy trigger fingers. But the young man in the pickup truck ignored both them and their guns.

They hesitated a moment in amazement and disbelief, then at a barked command, several of the officers dashed for their own vehicle and roared off in pursuit of the truck. They didn't try to stop it, but trailed the truck until it turned off the main road. Continuing, they followed it over a maze of bumpy trails, winding past fields of maize, sorghum, wheat, pumpkins, and tomatoes to a small isolated ranch a few miles south of the Rio Grande. There was no house on the property, but just a couple of sturdy sheds and a small corral. In the distance, the green shoots of young new crops were peeping through the black loam. It was the Santa Elena Ranch.

The driver's feet barely touched the ground as he slid from his seat in the cab before he was surrounded by the officers, their weapons held at the ready. Still, under the circumstances, he appeared strangely calm. he was a solidly-built young man with an unruly bristle of dark hair, and a stubble of whiskers that looked as if he had gone all day without shaving.

The sullen youth was armed with a .38-caliber pistol, but he made no effort to use it before it was roughly taken away. The officers also found a small amount of marijuana, just enough to spark their suspicions and return sometime later with a search warrant to take a closer look at the barren 100-acre spread. Their search turned up nearly seventy-pounds of the illegal weed.

Within a few hours four more men, in addition to the driver of the truck, had been taken into custody. The drug running suspects were identified through their own statements, or by personal papers they were carrying as: Twenty-year-old Serafin Hernandez Garcia; twenty-two-year-old Elio Hernandez Rivera; twenty-three-year-old Sergio Martinez Salinas; and twenty-three-year-old David Serna Valdez. The other prisoner rounded up in the rapidly burgeoning investigation was the caretaker, Domingo Reynes Bustamante. But unlike the others, Reyes was not charged with drug offenses. All the men except Hernandez Garcia, who lived in Brownsville and was the only member of the quintet who spoke English, said their homes were in Matamoros.

But the marijuana uncovered during the searches, and the subsequent arrests, weren't the most startling discoveries made by the squad of *federales*. After all, marijuana arrests were nothing unusual on the border. The contents of the storage shed were more curious. The darkened interior of the wood and tarpaper shed was littered with the wax stubs of burned votive candles, red peppers, empty bottles of Canoas rum, and the butts of La Palma cigars. There was also a makeshift altar holding small ceramic statues of Catholic saints, a scattering of rough clay bowls, some chalices, and, off to the side, a tin oil drum, and huge, black iron pots. The pots were coated with a malodorous smear of soot-blackened pale yellow grease.

Schooled in the superstitious legacy of their Indian and Spanish ancestors, the *federales* immediately realized what they had walked into. Quickly they left the hut, posted guards around the perimeter and notified their commandante, Juan Benitez Ayala, of their ominous discovery.

The young truck driver's reply when the *federales* demanded to know why he had speeded through the roadblock, was also strangely puzzling and intimidating. It was obvious that he wasn't drunk, and he didn't appear to be under the influence of drugs, but his cryptic reply made police wonder. He muttered something about being invisible.

A further search of the shed was called off until steps could be taken to deal with the intimidating supernatural forces that might be lingering around the area. A *shaman* was called in to cleanse the building and the immediate surrounding area of evil spirits. By the next afternoon it was considered safe to resume the search. And that's when the incident began evolving in earnest from a routine marijuana bust, into a deadly serious international investigation of drug running, kidnap, torture, and ritual murder.

In Brownsville, American authorities looking for Mark Kilroy had heard of the arrests at the ranch, and were pressing Benitez Ayala to check out the suspects for possible involvement with the missing college student. When a *federal* showed a photo of Kilroy to the ranch caretaker, he pulled the lid away from the ugly Pandora's box of crime and cultism surrounding the abduction.

"Yes," the caretaker said, "I saw him at the ranch one day." He had seen the blonde Gringo, bound and gagged in the back of a pickup truck in the parking area near the hut. And a few hours later, before being ordered to leave the ranch, he had fed the youth.

In light of the strong possibility that the men at the ranch were involved in Kilroy's disappearance, Lieutenant Gavito and Neck were invited to assist in the investigation. They found incredibly ghoulish evidence that, in addition to being used as a staging area for drug smuggling, some sort of eerie black magic rites had been carried out in the fourteen-by-twenty-one-foot shed.

The shed and it's environs had eventually yielded a total of 225 pounds of marijuana and 180 grams of cocaine, apparently ready for shipment across the border. There were also twelve high-powered weapons, and eleven cars and trucks equipped with sophisticated communications equipment. But drugs, sophisticated weaponry and fast cars and trucks especially outfitted with up-to-date communications equipment weren't new to the law enforcement agents who policed both sides of the border. A different, more malevolent kind of wickedness seemed to be present. The structure seemed to reek of mysterious evil and dark spirits.

The makeshift altar was splattered with blood and the melted remains of candles that had once been shaped with the likeness of Mexico's patron saint, Our Lady of Guadalupe. Flecks of rusty red stains that appeared to be blood were also spattered on the walls, and rough-edged sheets of plywood were stacked and tossed haphazardly on the floor. A pair of rusty wire coat-hangers hung twisted from a cross-beam. On the sill of a tiny window in the east corner of the shed, the *federales* found what appeared to be a bird's nest made from human hair. The glazed, frightened eyes of a goat stared unseeing at the *federales* from it's raggedly butchered head, propped up in a clay bowl. A bloody machete lay nearby.

But the most intriguing, and the most ominously disgusting contents of the shed were the large black iron cauldrons. They were encrusted with bloated green and blue blowflies and oozed with an oily soup consisting of blood, twigs, strange herbs, the feet, feathers and heads of roosters, turtle shells with rotting chunks of flesh still attached, yellow beads, hundreds of pennies, a horseshoe, railroad spikes and an ugly gray chunk of a curiously geletinous substance, that gray mass was human brain matter.

With kerchiefs pressed to their noses and mouths, the *federales* gingerly poked through the grisly, malodorous contents of the shed while other lawmen recorded shocking confessions from some of the drug-running suspects apprehended at the ranch.

The suspects had been stunned at their apprehension. They believed the promise of occult protection from arrest or harm, and appeared to be emotionally and mentally scrambled by the troubles into which they had been so suddenly dropped. They began blurting out a jarring story that was almost unbelievable in its deceit, stupidity and savagry.

Hernandez Garcia told his interrogators that he and two of his companions had kidnapped Mark and delivered him to the ranch — under the orders of the gang's godfather, a Cuban American they addressed as *El Padrino*, Godfather. The kidnapped college youth had been selected as a human sacrifice. One of the shaken suspects offered to lead investigators to the young man's grave.

As the squad of grim-faced lawmen, including Neck, were led toward the corral a few yards behind the shed, their prisoner pointed to a mound of soft earth just outside the rickety fence of the corral. The missing American student was buried there, he said. Then the prisoner turned and pointed to more graves, one after another. Neck later remarked to a reporter that the lawmen had been led into a killing field. The Customs agent was shaken. It was difficult to imagine the scene found at the ranch, he said. The law enforcement officers from the U.S. and Mexico had never seen anything like it.

A wire protruded from the dirt near one end of the first rectangular-shaped mound pointed out to the investigators. It marked Kilroy's grave. He had been murdered, mutilated, and his body covered with a few inches of loam and left to decay under the hot Mexican sun.

Discovery of Mark's remains was only the beginning of the nightmare uncovered at the ranch. Other suspicious mounds of earth were spotted throughout the area inside the corral, and a hundred-feet-or-so outside the fence near some piles of hay. Officers then began the grim job of exhuming additional bodies.

It was a grueling and gruesome chore made even worse by the blistering Mexican heat. Most of the bodies were recovered from three-to-four-foot graves within the corral near the sacrificial hut, barely deep enough to keep them from sight. The stench from the decaying flesh, as the remains were uncovered and slipped into body bags, was overpowering in the hot, moist air.

Some of the bodies had been beheaded; others had portions of their skulls intact, after being slashed open with machetes. Brains, hearts, and other internal organs had been torn and cut from the bodies.

The Mexican and U.S. media began converging on the ranch as soon as it was learned that Mark's body had been recovered. Some of the first hysterical reports of the nightmarish business carried out near Matamoros warned of frightening Satanic rites, spells to conjure up the devil, blood-drinking and cannibalism. The early reports were close, but not exact.

The hair-raising contents of the shed, and the pathetic condition of the rotting cadavers uncovered at the ranch made such hasty conclusions understandable, however. Blood, brains, and other human remains had, after all, been found in the cauldrons. And the flesh and blood had been used in some kind of evil religious rites that seemed to call for human sacrifice.

But the reports of cannibalism and Satanic rituals were squelched by investigators and by the suspects themselves. The cultists admitted that brains, blood, and other body parts had been cooked in a devil's stew with the herbs and animal remains. The ghastly mixture was not consumed by the cultists, however. The concoction was mixed as a feast for the gods.

Eventually, twelve bodies were pulled from fetid graves on the ranch. But interrogation of the suspects indicated that the law enforcement team hadn't yet recovered the remains of all the victims slaughtered there. One of the suspects who was talking, Martinez Salinas, was driven back to the ranch and ordered to point out the graves of victims still unrecovered. A Japanese film crew from a Tokyo-based television network, had just piled out of cars with their cameras when he pointed out one more soft rectangle of earth just behind a haystack. The suspect said he thought he remembered a body being buried there.

A ranking officer nodded at another of the *federales*, who stepped forward and shoved a shovel and a pickaxe into the stunned suspect's hands. He was surprised, and glanced at the tools uncertainly. He was ordered to dig.

"You'll do it with your hands if you have to," a *federale* threatened.

Grudgingly, as the uniformed policemen nervously cradled automatic rifles and looked on with a crowd of reporters and photographers, the young man began turning up the softly packed earth. It was obvious that the reluctant youth, hatless and dressed in blue jeans and a long-sleeved shirt, wasn't used to hard work. Although he had claimed that he was only a simple farm hand who worked at the bleak, one-hundred-acre ranch, there was no question that he was not a poor peon used to grubbing out the living by hard labor. When he started to dig, his hands were soft and uncalloused. Only a few shovelsful of earth had been lifted from the ground before his hands were blistered and sore. A few times he dropped the shovel and scooped out elusive chunks of dirt with his hands.

But as he bent industriously over the grave in the hot afternoon sun, there were no expressions of sympathy from the small crowd assembled to watch him work. As a knee and foot were uncovered and the first, fetid odors lifted from the decayed human flesh, Martinez Salinas recoiled, then gagged. Ignoring the machine guns held by the *federales*, he left the shovel sticking in the dirt and pleaded for a face mask. The stern expression on the faces of the *federales* never changed as they pointed the barrels of their weapons back to the grave and ordered Salinas to continue digging.

"You didn't need one when you buried him," one officer growled.

The *federales* didn't interfere, however, when a photographer handed the youth a scarf to put over his nose and mouth. But the unaccustomed labor, the heat, and the poisonous fumes released from the grave were taking their toll, and Martinas Salinas began to stagger. He pleaded for water, and seemed to be hardly able to lift the shovel. At last the *federales* allowed him to climb unsteadily from the grave, while two onlookers replaced him at the job of uncovering the body. When at last the victim was uncovered, investigators could see that although his head had been terribly mangled, it wasn't severed. A blindfold and gag were still in place. But the body was torn to pieces. The genitals were missing, and the chest had been slashed open and the heart ripped out, as if the victim had been an ancient Aztec sacrifice.

Still weak and wobbly after his brief rest, the sweat-soaked suspect was pressed back into service, and he and a helper used a rope tied to the bare feet of the corpse to pull it clear of the makeshift grave. That was the last of the victims to be found at the Santa Elena Ranch. All were males, twelve men and a boy.

Approximately a week after Martinez Salinas led police to the thirteenth body, two more victims of the killer cultists were recovered from the Ejido Santa Liberada, a collective farm just two miles south of the Santa Elena Ranch. Hidalgo Castillo summoned police to the gravesite among a stand of nopal cactus. After hearing of the terrible discoveries at the nearby Santa Elena Ranch, he had reluctantly decided that the story told by the children of someone being buried warranted closer investigation. The boys said they were chasing rabbits through a clearing in an orchard when they saw a hand sticking up from the soft earth.

Shortly before sunset, the heart-sick old man helped two workmen with shovels unearth the remains of his son, Moises Castillo Vasquez, and those of another. The hands and feet of the victims had been bound with rope, and their eyes covered. Both had been shot to death.

The bodies, now fragile and decomposing, had been dumped into a common grave, one on top of the other. Hidalgo Castillo sadly identified one of the corpses as his son. A pair of eyeglasses, seventy dollars in American money, and a U.S. passport were found with the remains.

Moise's companion in death was later identified as Hector de la Funete. Investigators found 3,000 Mexican pesos and a five dollar bill in the pockets of his rotting black trousers. De la Fuente's wife learned of his death while she was watching a television news broadcast.

The families were stunned by the tragedy. Moises Castillo's widow cried when she was questioned by news reporters. He had no enemies, only friends, she wept.

Hidalgo Castillo echoed his daughter-in-law's sentiments. He said he had no idea why his son was murdered — and that he had no enemies.

Public and official reaction to the nightmarish discovery at the Hell

Ranch was swift and predictable. Residents on both sides of the border recoiled in horror and anger.

Matamoros Mayor Fernando Montemayor Lozano and members of the Matamoros City Commission drafted an open letter to Mexico's new president, Carlos Salinas de Gortari. Printed in the Matamoros daily newspaper, *El Bravo,* the letter implored President Salinas to apply every available law to bring to justice the people responsible for invoking so much fear and uncertainty to the area.

Their pleas would not go unheard, or unheeded, by the president.

CHAPTER 8

Mutilation, Murder, and Magic

POLICE ON BOTH SIDES of the border had heard rumors and whispered stories about black magic cult activity among drug runners, but no one suspected anything like the horror uncovered at the Santa Elena Ranch.

However, they couldn't have been much more surprised at the disclosures and arrests than the four suspected cultists, Sergio Martinez Salinas, David Serna Valdez, Elio Hernandez Rivera, and Serafin Hernandez Garcia, Jr.

The quartet had been so certain of protection by the evil blood rites conducted at the ranch, that they were stunned and unbelieving when they were arrested. They were convinced that the dark spells they participated in had made exposure to police impossible. Their arrests were unthinkable.

Hadn't the Godfather assured them that they could never be caught? He had promised them in fact, that not only would they have the protection of invisibility, but they would be impervious to police bullets. The blood offerings to the dark gods worshipped and controlled by their leader were supposed to provide them with more protection than any corrupt policeman on the take could ever promise.

Yet, despite all the assurances of protection, and the terrible deeds they had participated in or condoned to please the blood-hungry gods, they suddenly found themselves captives of the police. Their newly-formed belief system had collapsed, and they weren't emotionally or mentally prepared for the shock.

Hernandez Garcia, his cousin Elio, and their companions were marched in handcuffs to the second floor of the Federal Judicial Police Headquarters in Matamoros. There, under the cold and watchful eyes of *Comandante* Benitez Ayala, they spoke in monotones to a large crowd of reporters from the United States and Mexico, calmly detailing their roles — and the roles of others — in the nine-month-long blood feast at the ranch.

The spectacle of such a public questioning of suspects could never have happened in the United States, where laws and civil libertarians are more protective of the accused.

But the suspects were in Mexico. And as they chatted with police and the press about the crimes, huge earth movers and back hoes, loaned by private firms in the United States, were working in a steady drizzle of rain in the search for still more bodies at the two ranches where some remains had already been found. Other workmen ripped jagged, muddy gashes in the earth with heavy machinery at Rancho Caracol, another property owned by Hernandez family members about fifty-miles southeast of Matamoros. But no additional bodies were found at any of the ranches.

Those that were recovered earlier were taken to local funeral homes, where Mexican pathologists began the somber task of conducting autopsies. Distraught relatives of missing men who rushed to one of the funeral homes as soon as they learned of the ghastly discoveries were gently turned away, and advised to go first to the federal police headquarters. "We need time to wash the corpses and get them ready for burial," one mortician somberly explained.

The suspects talked easily to the reporters, as they had talked to police interrogators, about drug running, black magic, human sacrifice and gangland killings. And they named their leaders.

Speaking of the sacrificial victims, Elio told reporters: "We killed them for protection." Later, without pinpointing the specific gang members he was accusing, Elio offered a slightly amended version of his statement. "They killed him to get more protection," he said.

In yet another version explaining the dreadful atrocities that occurred at the ranch, Elio said that he shot and killed one victim and decapitated another. Speaking almost casually, the suspects confirmed that human sacrifice was part of their religion. They believed the rites were necessary to make them invincible.

Serafin Hernandez Garcia told a reporter that he thought the clan followed a good religion when he joined. He said that by the time he realized that people were being murdered, it was too late to get out.

Although not confessing to committing any of the murders, twenty-three-year-old Sergio Martinez Salinas told the reporters, "I'm guilty. I was ordered to dig the graves and bury (Kilroy)." Sergio was a quiet spoken, polite and pleasant appearing young man whom other gang members referred to as "La Mariposa." In English "La Mariposa" is translated as "The Butterfly," and in Mexico the slightly derogatory term is used to denote a homosexual.

Hernandez Garcia, the only son of the four to speak fluent English, denied participating in any of the slayings and blamed *El Padrino* for Kilroy's murder.

El Padrino was identified during police interrogations as a young American of Cuban ancestry, Adolfo de Jesus Constanzo. They said he was not only the ringleader and mastermind of the drug running killer cult, but he either performed the slayings himself, or directed them.

Sara Maria Aldrete Villarreal, the deceptively sweet and studious coed from Texas Southmost College, was also implicated during the first rush of confessions from the dumbfounded suspects. They identified her as the cult's Witch, or high priestess. But none of the suspects, not even the ranch caretaker, could lead police to the pair. The last they had been heard from was a few hours before the police raid, when they were at the Brownsville Holiday Inn with other gang members. But police quickly confirmed that the fugitives had gone underground.

Police said several of the suspected drug cultists were still on the loose. And they identified one of the suspects still being sought, and possibly accompanying Constanzo and Sara, as Alvaro de Leon Valdez, the reputedly kill-crazy *pistolero* from Matamoros.

In Brownsville, U.S. Customs agent Oran Neck said the gang was believed to have been smuggling about a ton of marijuana across the border each week. He added that the Constanzo-led smugglers were also apparently a larger drug trafficking ring than previously thought. "There could be two or three dozen members," he advised.

Neck said that the gang members lived wealthy lifestyles. And none who were suspects in the cult slayings at that time, had criminal records. Neck said that several additional agents from the DEA had been detailed to work in the Brownsville area on the rapidly burgeoning case.

The Customs officer made a special point of complimenting the work of Mexico's often criticized Federal Judicial Police in the case. And he had special praise for Benitez Ayala's performance in helping to clear up the Kilroy disappearance and break up the drug smuggling gang.

Cameron County Sheriff's Lieutenant Gavito agreed with the praise of the Federal Judicial Police and of Benitez Ayala. He said that none of the other police agencies in Mexico aided to help find the missing college student, only the FJP and Benitez.

Contrary to the historic attitude of many high-ranking Mexican police officers, Benitez Ayala modestly shied away from the firestorm of publicity, and insisted that all the officers who worked on the case be given proper credit. He told one reporter that he was getting all the glory, but that as Commandante he could not have accomplished anything without the loyalty and determination of the officers he commanded.

And he stressed that the difficult job facing Federal Judicial Police had not ended with the breakup of the cultists. Drug smuggling was still endemic along the border, and only the previous week federal police had arrested five men after they were stopped at the Valle Hermoso checkpoint, reputedly attempting to smuggle more than 130 pounds of marijuana across the border.

At about the same time, other federal police officers picked up four men and a woman in Matamoros and charged them with possession, after they were allegedly found with more than 260 pounds of marijuana, two rifles and two nine-millimeter pistols. Benitez Ayala vowed that the fight would go on.

Based on confessions and on other evidence, the members of the quartet were charged with first-degree murder, kidnapping, drug trafficking, violation of federal burial and exhumation laws, criminal conspiracy, and impersonating federal officials. The caretaker was initially accused of helping cover up the gang's crimes for failing to report illegal activities at the ranch, but it was rapidly determined that he had never been a participant and he was released from custody on low bail. No bail was set for the others.

As the prisoners in Matamoros continued to add details about their grim activities, police were astonished at the widespread misery inflicted in such a short time by the enigmatic cultists who mixed kidnapping, mutilation, sex and murder with drug running. It was a tale more unbelievable and more terrifying than any horror or slasher movie. Yet it was all true, and it had happened in and near Matamoros.

The story the prisoners told sent chills down the spines of the most hardened police officers. Craftily taking advantage of their superstitious beliefs, Constanzo had become lord over a group of young men of some privilege, who did anything he asked. He promised them wealth beyond their wildest imaginings and protection from police and rival gangs. But the promise carried a heavy price — the cold-blooded murder and mutilation of innocent men in a nightmare ritual that would have sickened most normal persons.

Amazingly, even though they were at last in police custody, the four suspects were still convinced that Constanzo's loathsome magic would protect them. According to a newspaper report, Elio was so cocky that he challenged Commandante Benitez to shoot him. "Go ahead. Your bullets will just bounce off," he was quoted as boasting.

Elio Hernandez even bragged about the cryptic occult symbols, crosses and arrows, branded on his arm, chest and back with a red-hot knife used by Constanzo to mark him as an executioner priest. Another gang member nicknamed "El Duby" and thought to be on the run with Constanzo, had similar marks, the prisoners revealed.

They showed no remorse for the vicious acts they were accused of committing or condoning. They had joked and giggled as they led police to the graves of the men murdered on the Hell Ranch, and they talked unhesitatingly about other cult members, apparently in the warped, mistaken belief that everything would be all right.

Investigators were grim and their faces faded to a pallid gray in reaction to the breath-taking contempt for human life indicated by the suspects as they recounted monotonous tales of murder, mutilation and human sacrifice.

The charismatic Cuban had his followers wholly convinced that they would have complete protection if they prayed to and fed the ghoulish demands of his gods, in ceremonies that were fashioned from a bizarre mishmash of the worst aspects of the African and Caribbean pagan religions of *Santeria,* Voodoo and *Palo Mayombe,* along with a strong dose of black magic and Mexican folk beliefs.

The cultists believed so strongly in their enigmatic leader and his reputed supernatural powers that they carried out his every order without question, even kidnapping innocent men and boys for human sacrifice. They couldn't deny that their drug smuggling operation had prospered and their earnings mushroomed since *El Padrino* had taken over. And if he credited their success with protection he had attracted from occult forces, then it must be true.

Questioning of the suspects brought out stories of unprecedented brutality and horror — like the killings of twenty-two-year-old Victor Saul Sauceda and fourteen-year-old Jose Luis Garcia Luna.

The gang was preparing to move a ton of marijuana across the Rio Grande about a mile from the ranch, when *El Padrino* advised that the gods would demand a blood sacrifice to protect the shipment and the smugglers. Sauceda, a fiery-tempered, ex-Matamoros policeman, was selected as the victim.

Sauceda was no stranger to trouble, and had reputedly resigned from the police department in September 1986, after his cousin, Brigido Sauceda, was killed. Victor had been a policeman only four months, and the reason he felt it necessary to resign after Brigido's death was never fully explained. But he was being seen with members of the Constanzo gang, and there was talk that he had moved from law enforcement to law breaking.

Late in March 1989, while he was employed at an auto parts and repair shop in Matamoros, he had a run in with his former boss from the police department. Police said that Sauceda was speeding and nearly hit the officer's car, leading to a chase. The chase ended when Sauceda skidded to a stop and dashed inside a private home, where police couldn't follow. Several days later, on April 1, he was on an errand for his boss when he disappeared. Someone reported he had been seen climbing into a Matamoros police car. Some of his associates began deliberating the possibilities that enemies in the police department may have had something to do with his disappearance.

It wasn't until Sauceda's body was dug up at the farm that his family and others learned for sure that he hadn't been killed by corrupt police. And there were indications that Sauceda may have died because he had been working as an undercover drug agent assigned to infiltrate the Constanzo gang. No one in authority among Mexican police agencies, at this writing, has yet stepped forward to clear up Sauceda's exact relationship to the gang.

But Sauceda was believed to be working, either as a policeman, private detective or clandestine informant, on the slaying in July 1988 of Lauro Martinez and his friend at Los Sombreros.

For whatever reason Sauceda found himself at the Santa Elena Ranch, as part of an undercover effort to collar the killer of two young men at the Sombrero Bar, because he witnessed the execution of a local cocaine dealer or, as yet other stories suggested, as part of a drug deal that ended in a doublecross — he was handpicked by Constanzo to become a human sacrifice.

Sauceda was no naive young boy who was ready to surrender his life meekly, and when he realized what was going on he pulled a gun. But he had barely moved the weapon from his waistband before he was overpowered. Then he was tortured, horribly. According to an account later attributed to Rivera by police, the tough ex-cop refused to beg for mercy or to scream, even when Constanzo sliced off one of his ears. So the torture was continued, slowly and deliberately. His flesh was repeatedly stabbed, slashed and gouged in inhuman acts of nightmarish ferocity. Commandante Benitez later told reporters that Saucedo had been skinned alive.

The Godfather was stimulated by the act of killing, and it seemed to his followers that he became another being. His words slurred together, and his body trembled with orgiastic pleasure. He loved the power. Sometimes he killed with the machete, sometimes with a hammer or a knife. And at other times, he used his hands to snap the neck of his helpless victims.

Saucedo didn't manage to escape death, but he had evaded becoming a human sacrifice whose life could be presented to the gods in a carefully proscribed death ritual. In doing so, however, he doomed another young man to a horrible death. Another male would have to be found quickly, to be ritually offered to the gods so that the marijuana could be moved across the border with supernatural protection. Three of the cultists left the ranch, and a short distance away happened on Jose Luis Garcia Luna as he was looking for a cow that had wandered from its pasture.

Jose and his family lived just around a curve on National Highway 40, leading into the west side of Matamoros, and were well-known among neighbors who worked on the ranches and communal farms, or *ejidos*, in the area. He was the youngest of seven children, and only three weeks earlier had taken a job at a nearby ranch, Villa Hermosa, tending cows in order to help with family finances.

But the kidnappers hardly glanced at the startled boy before throwing a gunnysack over his head and roughhousing him into a pickup truck. The abduction was accomplished in moments. It took the cultists only a few minutes to drive to the Santa Elena Ranch with their captive.

The boy was hurried into the rust-colored death shack with his hands tied behind him and the gunnysack still pulled over his head. The cauldron had been prepared, and Elio was waiting to fulfill his function as an executioner priest. The cultists gathered in a semi-circle around the frightened boy, their bodies casting weirdly elongated shadows on the walls of the shed in the candlelight. As Elio mumbled an incantation, he raised a razor-sharp machete over his shoulder, then slashed the boy's head from his body with a single savage swing.

Blood spurted from the child's severed neck as the headless body fell to the orange tarpaulin covering the sacrificial circle. That was when Elio first noticed the telltale gray and green football jersey the boy was wearing. Even Elio was shaken as he reached into the sack and pulled out the grisly head of his cousin, but the ritual had to be carried out to conclusion. Reaching into the boy's shattered skull, the death priest removed his still-warm brain and placed it in the *n'ganga* as an offering to the gods. Returning to the body, the executioner priest lifted the football jersey and slashed open the chest. The lungs were removed and placed in the murky brew in the *n'ganga,* alongside the brain.

That evening, Isidorio Garcia Benavidez and his wife, Ericada Garcia, spent hours looking for their missing son. No one at the Villa Hermosa had seen him since he set off looking for the stray. They walked the Calle-Hidalgo, the tree-lined main street of Lucio Blanco, a tiny town three or four miles south of the Santa Elena Ranch, where everyone knew them. They searched for days, and left photographs of their boy with police in Matamoros and at the police station on the town square in Lucio Blanco. Commander Servando Sanchez Rivera posted the boy's photo on a wall above his desk. The couple, as devoutly evangelical as the Kilroys are devoutly Catholic, were equally determined to find their lost boy, although they had neither the resources or the know-how of the couple who would soon become their Texas counterparts. But like the search that would later be set in motion by the Kilroys, the Mexican couple's search was doomed to failure. No one came forward who had seen the missing fourteen-year-old. And unlike the international hunt initiated by the Kilroys, the heartbroken farming couple's anguished search would attract no publicity until their son was found.

Jose Luis Garcia de Luna had been a victim of chance, incredible bad luck, as Mark would be later. The human sacrifices were a freakish new development in the drug cult's peculiar method of operation. Most of the bodies found at the ranches belonged to men such as Moises Castillo Vasquez and Hector de la Fuente, believed to have died as the result of drug dealing double-crosses or unforgivable bungling.

And Sauceda wasn't the only victim with known police connections. One of the bodies dug up at the ranch was that of Valentin del Fierro, who also used the name Pedro Gloria. He was a former *Madrina,* an informant said to have been in tight with Tamilipas state police. Another was Gilberto

Garza, a twenty-year-old ex-Matamoros policeman who was nicknamed, "El Lechero," The Milkman. Milkmen make deliveries, and corrupt police are known to use low-ranking officers to pick up bribes and to carry information back-and-forth to criminals about drug deals or movement of marijuana.

Commandante Benitez laconically pointed out to reporters that the gang had apparently realized it was easier and cheaper to steal and kill for drugs than it was to pay greedy suppliers. Consequently, the youthful drug smugglers would negotiate with suppliers, then lure them to the ranch where they would be killed and mutilated. The bodies would be disposed of in shallow graves, and the drugs — which they had never paid for — would then be smuggled across the river with as much ease as had been employed in the murder of the original owners.

After interrogation of the prisoners and through other investigation, police disclosed that twenty-seven-year-old Ezequiel Rodriguez Luna, of Matamoros, and two associates apparently were victims of the gang's ruthless double-cross. Rodriguez was believed to be leader of a small band which had a ton of marijuana to sell, and after contacting Constanzo, took three of *El Padrino*'s men to a warehouse where the contraband was stored. Thirty-year-old Ruben Vela Garza was guarding the cache, possibly with another man.

Constanzo's gang members weren't satisfied with the quality of the marijuana, and complained about the price. Rodriguez insisted that they pay his price, so the cultists telephoned *El Padrino*. He instructed them to kidnap Rodriguez and his associates and bring them to the ranch. And they were told to steal the marijuana.

Vela Garza was armed and acted like he knew how to use his weapon, so Constanzo's group left peacefully. But a short time later they showed up with about a dozen other men at Vela Garza's house in La Pesca, a few miles outside Matamoros, in a blue suburban and a smaller car. They were heavily armed and claimed to be police agents as they forced Vela Garza and a companion, twenty-three-year-old Ernesto Rivas Diaz, a welder from Monterrey, into the cars.

The group drove into Matamoros, where they picked up Rodriguez at his home near the Los Pinos Bowling Alley, and shoved him into one of the cars. All three of the prisoners were bound and gagged and driven to the Santa Elena Ranch. There they were marched to a ditch already dug in the black earth, pushed inside and machine-gunned to death. There was no one to stop the cultists when they drove back to the warehouse and loaded up the marijuana.

There were some indications that one or more of the trio may have been tortured or sacrificed before being dumped into the ditch. The cause of death listed on Rivas Diaz's death certificate was "irreversible lesion to a vital organ" — his brain.

Medical examiners determined that another of the victims, Gilberto Garza Sosa, died from hemorrhage after numerous blows to the body. A spokesman for the narcotics division of the federal district attorney's office disclosed that Garza Sosa was a known drug trafficker who was linked to an organized drug smuggling ring. Sosa, who lived in Brownsville and had worked as a railroad security guard, was tortured before he was killed, in what police said was apparently a drug deal gone sour.

But there were other even nastier stories about the thirty-seven-year-old Sosa's death as well. It was said that the married man had carried on a romance with *La Madrina*, and that she and the gang had turned on him — possibly because of a fallout with Sara, and, according to other accounts, because he had welched on payment of money he owed to Constanzo. Whatever the motive, when his pitifully mutilated body was unearthed at the Santa Elena Ranch, he had been castrated, one of his small toes cut off, a nipple sliced from his chest, and his neck broken. Sara would later vehemently deny reports of a romance, and any hints that she had participated in the torture of a former lover or of anyone else.

Most of the bodies lifted from the fetid black earth were in such bad shape, and the memories of the suspects so spotty, that details were sometimes vague, but always their stories were dominated by horror. It wasn't always possible to determine if some of the bodies had been mutilated by torture, chopped and cut up after death, or merely decomposed. One of the victims was said to have had his heart torn from his chest while he was still alive. Another had his face still twisted in horror, and there was talk that he had been scalded alive. The cultists had reveled in fear and pain. Their rituals were a banquet of blood.

Journalists were working a big story and they squeezed it for every inch of newspaper copy, every possible minute on the nightly news. Family members and neighbors of suspects and victims were tracked down and interviewed, over and over again. Law enforcement officers on both sides of the border, and survivors of the victims were repeatedly questioned, and experts on criminology, perverse psychology, and cults were sought out and asked to help provide insight into the horror at the ranch and into Constanzo's Manson-like ability to attract followers and command their unswerving loyalty.

James Alan Fox, a criminal justice professor in Boston and an authority on mass murder, said that Constanzo fit neatly into the tradition of recent cult leaders. "Like Charles Manson and Jim Jones, he convinced normal people to do crazy things," the professor noted.

A high-ranking Mexican government official, who agreed to comment if he was not named, declared: "The blind loyalty of the band to Constanzo was like the Nazi admiration of Hitler during World War II. He was their father figure, and he could do no wrong."

Carl Raschke, who teaches world religions at the University of Denver was quoted in *People* magazine as saying that religious ideology was used almost like corporate motivational training to hold criminal gangs together and to enforce obedience.

The Mexican mother of one of the victims at Hell Ranch said that Constanzo was evil and that his followers willingly allowed themselves to be seduced by promises of riches. "He was *El Satanás*, Satan," she whispered, crossing herself and muttering a hasty prayer to the Virgin Mother.

In Texas, Helen Kilroy's reaction was similar to that of the Mexican mother. "I think the people who killed Mark and the others must be possessed by the devil," she said at an early news conference. "That's the only explanation I have for what they did."

Speaking at the same gathering, Mark's younger brother, Keith, observed that drug smugglers and black magic cultists are not unique to Mexico. "It could happen in my own town," he said.

In "My Turn," a guest column in the *Brownsville Herald*, Pastor Mark Stanton of the New Life Center United Pentecostal Church, tied the slaughter to the erosion of Judeo-Christian morals by the rising tide of humanism. He wrote that it was difficult to understand why people would be surprised by the grisly discoveries outside Matamoros, or shocked to learn that devil worship had been taking place in their community.

On April 17, exactly one week after the bodies were discovered at the Hell Ranch, DEA agents in Houston arrested one more member of the Hernandez family. Forty-five-year-old Serafin Hernandez Rivera was jailed without bond on a series of drug offense charges outlined in an indictment returned earlier by a federal grand jury in McAllen.

Serafin Hernandez Rivera was the father of one of the suspects, Serafin Hernandez Garcia, and the older brother of another, the reputed executioner priest, Elio Hernandez Rivera. A few weeks after his arrest, Serafin Hernandez Rivera, the only member of the reputed gang apprehended on U.S. soil, was transferred for trial to Brownsville, where he was jailed just across the Gateway International Bridge from his son and brother.

Although the newest prisoner was accused of working with other members of the gang to smuggle and distribute drugs, authorities quickly pointed out that he was not a suspect in any of the cult murders. "There's no reason to believe he's involved in that part of it," Neck said of the gruesome sacrificial slayings.

The four suspects who were accused of involvement in the slaughter were expected to have a difficult time clearing themselves in the courts. Mexico follows the Napoleonic Code, now called the Civil Code, which was enacted in 1804. Unlike the U.S. judicial system which operates with the predication that criminal defendants are innocent until proven guilty, simply put, according to Mexican criminal codes defendants are presumed guilty until they prove themselves not guilty.

Whatever the conclusion of the legal processes might be, the accused drug-cult killers were assured of better treatment than their victims. Mexico has no death penalty. Nor does the criminal code provide for cumulative sentences, so there is no possibility that penalties can be stacked and run to hundreds of years of prison time. The most serious crime they could be charged with and convicted of is aggravated homicide, which carries a maximum fifty-year-prison term.

Uncovering the graves at the ranch.

Evidence of Satanic rituals.

Santa Elena Ranch

CHAPTER 9

The Death of Mark Kilroy

MARK KILROY DIED BECAUSE he was a victim of circumstances. He died because he had blonde hair and Anglo good looks. He died because he happened to be in the wrong place at the wrong time, according to the people responsible for his murder.

The boyishly handsome student was a marked man from the moment he acknowledged the salutation from the mysterious, English-speaking Mexican in downtown Matamoros. That man and three others were under orders from *El Padrino*, Adolfo de Jesus Constanzo, to find a young, healthy Gringo male as a sacrifice to the dark forces that they believed protected them from the police and rival gangs.

Mark, fair-haired and muscular from years of school athletics, seemed like the ideal candidate for the Godfather's evil plan, and the men, riding in a pickup and a car, stalked him like hungry jungle cats.

The unsuspecting pre-med student probably could have escaped Mexico with his life had he and his friend, Bill Huddleston, continued walking toward the bridge leading to the U.S. border. Unfortunately it wasn't to be. Feeling a call of nature, Bill ducked down a darkened side alley to find a private place to relieve himself, leaving Mark — disoriented from a night of guzzling beer — alone for just enough time for the hunters to close in.

Bill later told police that he was gone no more than two or three minutes, but it was time enough for the four men to snatch his friend and drag him into the night.

The leader of the kidnap team was twenty-year-old Serafin Hernandez Garcia, a wiry, chubby-faced middle-class youth who had graduated from Nimitz High School in Houston the same year Mark Kilroy graduated from Santa Fe High. Like Mark, Serafin had played high school baseball, but apart from that coincidence, the two boys could hardly have been more different.

Whereas Mark was clean-cut, dedicated and secure in his firm Christian faith, Serafin had become accustomed to the rich, flashy and risky lifestyle that drug smuggling provided. He liked the excitement, the money, fast cars, and fancy clothes. And while it might be debatable if the gang's success

82

was a direct result of Constanzo's bastard hybrid religion, he couldn't deny that profits were up and his lifestyle better than ever since the enigmatic Cuban had entered his life. So when Constanzo ordered him to find a Gringo to appease the gods, Serafin didn't argue. He just did what had to be done.

The kidnappers' ploy was deceptively simple: Serafin, standing next to the pickup truck, merely called to Mark in English. When Mark stepped closer to talk to the young Mexican, he was grabbed and roughly pushed into the truck's cab and securely stuffed between Serafin and another gang member. The kidnapping happened so quickly and was carried out so smoothly that passersby on the neon-lighted street didn't notice anything at all.

Even though his senses may have been dulled from alcohol, Mark probably put up a spunky fight inside the cramped truck cab. He was a muscular 175-pounds and a sturdy six-foot, two-inches, that he kept in fighting trim with regular exercise and good food. But although he kicked and attempted to strike at his attackers with his fists according to his captors, the odds were against him. He was easily subdued.

The sounds of music, laughter and hubbub on the busy Avenida Alvaro Obregon, where revellers were heading back to the Gateway International Bridge after a night of partying, were beginning to fade in the distance when Serafin stopped the truck near the Del Prado Hotel about three blocks down the road to urinate. Allegedly the scrappy young Texan realized that he had one more chance to escape, and he started fighting again. He managed to bull his way out of the truck, and bolted away.

Mark ran as fast as he could, but the uneven contest ended abruptly when gang members, serving as the rear guard, piled out of their car and cut him off. David Serna Valdez and another cultist grabbed him and rough-housed him back to the car, and this time they tied his hands and blindfolded him before tossing him into the back seat for the ride to the Santa Elena Ranch, some twenty miles outside Matamoros.

The bumpy ride to the cult's isolated home-base was a slow one that took the kidnappers and their helpless victim through the grimy backstreets of Matamoros and past the industrial section where a sizeable percentage of the city's population earned their living. As the mini-convoy moved out of the city, shadowy buildings gradually gave way to freshly tilled produce fields beautifully illuminated by a quarter moon.

Mark's mop of fashionably trimmed shoulder-length blonde hair unmistakably marked him as an Anglo, and that's exactly what his kidnappers had been looking for. When Mark's friends learned later of the bizarre selection process, they were stunned. It seemed that they too may have been stalked by the cultists, and any one of them could just as easily been singled out and snatched away when their defenses were weak. But it was Mark who was left alone and vulnerable for a moment, and that seemingly insignificant move cost him his life.

Once out of Matamoros, according to testimony, the gang drove down one dusty Mexican road after another before turning onto a narrow trail that cleaved through a corn field. At the end of the road was a barn with farm equipment on one side and an irrigation levee on the other. It was their destination: the Santa Elena Ranch.

Mark's kidnappers ushered the terrified college student from the car, reapplied his blindfold more securely with fresh strips of duct tape and placed him in a dirty barn where the cult stored marijuana. The men tried to calm and reassure Mark, promising that he wouldn't be harmed, then left to contact Constanzo to tell him that his orders to provide an Anglo for sacrifice had been carried out.

The Godfather was staying at the Brownsville Holiday Inn when his followers telephoned. They had followed his commands perfectly. A young Anglo Spring Breaker had been abducted. His intelligence and healthy body would make a proper offering to enlist the protection of the blood-hungry Afro-Caribbean gods.

The suspects gave the following account to the police of the grisly ritual.

Later that morning Constanzo arrived at the ranch, and began preparing for the grisly ritual he was so certain would please his followers — as well as the gods — and increase his power and authority. Entering the darkened shack, he inspected the altar. It had been set up with small ceramic figurines of Catholic saints, lighted candles, a chalice, and seven strips of colored cloth — to represent the seven African powers. Constanzo added a handful of black cigars, a newly opened bottle of cheap Mexican rum, and filled several small clay bowls with mysterious liquids, powders, and herbs. Some wrinkled, red chili peppers were meticulously sprinkled on and near the altar.

About two o'clock that afternoon, as the cultists were making ready for the sacrifice, a caretaker at the ranch was directed to prepare a final meal for Mark, of bread, eggs, and water. The caretaker scrambled the eggs and put them on a plate with a piece of bread. Then he filled a glass with tepid water, and left the area.

Still blindfolded, Mark was removed from the stifling, tin-roofed storage barn, and alternately pulled and shoved to a nearby 14-by-21-foot hut with red tarpaper walls. He was allowed to eat outside the hut, still unaware that it was his last meal. He slumped fearfully against the shed, sitting on the bare ground awkwardly feeding himself with his bound hands.

Inside the shack, the preparations for his death had been completed.

Police later speculated that sometime after finishing his eggs and bread, Mark may have realized that he was about to be murdered and made a last-ditch run for his life, despite the fact that he was blindfolded with tape. He was surrounded by cultists, however, and they were heavily armed with guns and knives. They quickly ran him down, and at gunpoint he was dragged into the killing shed. The cruel charade was over.

After forcing Mark into the hut, the Godfather ordered some of his followers to wait outside while he and specially selected acolytes performed the bloody sacrifice. Two of those later said to have joined him in the shed were Elio Hernandez Rivera, whom *El Padrino* had already ordained as an executioner priest by branding him with the tell-tale arrow symbols from the white-hot tip of a knifeblade, and Alvaro de Leon Valdez, "El Duby," who had become another of the leaders chief lieutenants.

If anything at all good can be said about Mark's ritual execution, it must be that it was swift, and presumably, relatively painless. He wasn't tortured or mutilated before he was killed.

Dressed in a flowing white robe and wearing a necklace of multicolored beads, Constanzo raised his arms before the altar, and with carefully measured movements lighted one of the cigars. Bending slightly, he blew the smoke in Mark's face. Then he took a swig from the bottle of rum, and a moment later spewed the fiery drink over the youth. There was a brief whispering of strange words that were neither English, nor Spanish, before he turned and forced the terrified college student to kneel over an orange tarpaulin.

Beads of sweat glistened on *El Padrino*'s forehead in the devilish candlelight. In a husky voice that was almost a croak, the Godfather muttered another invocation, summoning unseen deities. There was a moment of hushed anticipation as fragments of faces loomed in the flickering gloom of the shack like misshapen demons. Then the heavy blade of a machete slashed down onto the back of Mark's head, slicing off a ragged chunk of tissue and bone. The ungodly meeting of the machete and the boy's skull made a popping sound. The cultists, who watched silently, later said it sounded like a ripe coconut being split open.

Mark died instantly. Blood was still spurting from his severed neck as Constanzo bent over the corpse and scooped the brain, steaming from body heat, into his hands and slid the slippery mass into a ritual bowl. Cultists waiting outside were summoned into the infernal abattoir. Obediently, they filed into the blurred darkness of the hut and began chanting sonorous prayers over the bowl and it's hideous contents.

Once more the Godfather picked up the dripping brain, transferring it to a larger, gore-caked metal cauldron that already held a gut-churning brew of blood, herbs, rooster feet, feathers, goat heads, and other animal parts. With a fustian flourish, Constanzo raised his arms and began chanting over the bubbling, crimson mixture as the brain boiled and popped and his followers stood, trance-like, at the darkened perimeter of the light, their senses dulled by beer, cheap Mexican liquor, and horror.

Constanzo revelled in the grotesque ritual sacrifices. Each act of sanguine horror made him loom more powerful and omnipotent to the others who so blindly followed him.

As the smoke from the sacrificial cauldron containing Mark's flesh billowed around him, the Godfather's eyes widened in feral excitement and his speech seemed to grow more gutteral and unearthly. Weird, half-human shadows formed and twisted sinuously on the dark walls, the vague outlines changing constantly as the candle flames and the flickering tendrils of fire under the cauldron took on devilish shapes. Praying and chanting, the Godfather's voice raised in an animal-like whine, and his eyes flashed like yellow lightning. He seemed to magically grow larger and stronger while his followers watched, their faces pallid and slack with fascination and fear.

The grotesque ceremony continued, as *El Padrino* and his followers attacked and brutalized Mark's body again and again, severing his genitals and ripping out his heart. (The youth's body would be so grossly mutilated before the orgiastic frenzy subsided that police and pathologists were later unable to be completely certain of his identity until they compared his jaws and teeth with dental records sent to Matamoros by his dentist.) Even then, the orgy of murder and mutilation wasn't complete.

"El Duby" later admitted to police that he had been frightened during Mark's slaying because it was the first ceremonial execution he had participated in. Queerly, his fright didn't begin to subside until Constanzo ordered him to cut Mark's legs off.

"Do this and your fear will go away," *El Padrino* promised.

Dutifully, "El Duby" took the bloodied machete from his leader and used it to sever Mark's legs at mid-calf. With the blistering mid-day heat beating on the tin roof, the interior of the shack was stifling. The rotting odor of decomposing flesh and blood from the clotted devils' brew already fouling the cauldrons was overpowering, smothering. And cutting through bone with a machete was difficult. "El Duby's" shirt was caked to his body with sweat, and his broad shoulders were heaving when he finally accomplished his gruesome assignment. But he was pleased. He had earned his stripe as an executioner priest.

Severing Mark's legs was not part of the ritual. Constanzo ordered the revoltingly necrophilic act to make burial easier and to bind de Leon Valdez closer to him.

El Padrino told his exhausted acolyte that Christians were animals, and they could only be purified by becoming sacrificial offerings to the gods. And he said that when one of his followers earned his stripe, signified by the mark branded on his body, that the new priest's soul died.

By his own later admission, de Leon Valdez enjoyed the blood letting, and later pleaded with *El Padrino* to allow him to officiate at human sacrifices. Constanzo however reserved that privilege for himself, and later for Elio Hernandez Rivera. The Matamoros *pistolero* was permitted only to take an active part in the torture and post-mortem mutilation. He sliced off the fingers of victims. "El Duby" was anxious to do anything that would help him share *El Padrino*'s magical powers.

His blood lust sated at last, Constanzo ordered his henchmen to drive a length of thin wire through Mark's spinal column. Then, Serafin Hernandez Garcia carried the pathetically mangled remains from the nightmarish charnel house to a nearby corral just yards from the shack. Sergio Martinez, "La Mariposa," had already scooped out a shallow grave, and Mark's body was dumped inside and covered up. The wire was left protruding from the bone-dry black dirt like a freakish grave marker so that the cultists could find Mark's body after his flesh had rotted away. A simple tug on the wire would enable them to pull out the vertebra to wear as a macabre ceremonial necklace for extra protection and good luck.

When Mark's parents learned of the terrible manner of his death, week's after the repulsive business at the shack was concluded, they were heartsick at the ferocity of the act. But they were comforted when they were told that several hours had passed between the time of their eldest son's abduction and his murder. And they indicated that despite Mark's agony and theirs, they did not hold malice against his abusers.

"I think they must be possessed by the devil," Helen Kilroy said. "That can be the only explanation for what they did. I pray for all of them."

"Mark had plenty of time to cry out for God's help," his father, James Kilroy quietly observed. "When you cry out, God listens."

Mark Kilroys funeral service

CHAPTER 10

Dark Rites

ALDOFO DE JESUS CONSTANZO used the dark side of religion to maintain a firm hold on his weak-willed followers, but it wasn't any religion in particular. Instead, Constanzo used elements from several bizarre religious faiths, including *Santeria,* Voodoo, *Palo Mayombe* and traditional Mexican Witchcraft, commonly known as *Brujeria.* And there were dark hints in his rituals of ancient Aztec human sacrifice, as well.

"This is an instance where someone has brought with him a body of knowledge and used the theatrics and other ritual practices to engage and eventually enslave the minds of young people who are members of his cult," TSC's anthropology Professor Dr. Tony Zavaleta, an expert in cult religions, told newsmen.

"It took a strong, charismatic person who can only work his business by enslaving people to do his will."

The kind of power exhibited by Constanzo over his followers made work for the police even harder.

"Among cult members, there is a lot of loyalty inspired by fear, but not in the usual way," a narcotics investigator for the Texas Department of Public Safety explained. "They truly believe the leader has power over them after death. So they're not afraid of law officers or dying. That's something we really have to think about."

In the end, however, it was the money that proved Constanzo a superior leader — riches that were supposedly acquired with the help and protection of blood-thirsty gods with an insatiable appetite for human flesh.

There was no denying that the gang was prospering financially — the constant flow of illegal drugs into the U.S. meant a growing, seemingly endless supply of American dollars for everyone. The good times resumed for the drug smugglers when Constanzo first ordered his gang members to pray to demonic gods. There was no denying his success! Constanzo was their connection to, admittedly blood-drenched, life in the fast lane. If it meant the occasional brutal murder and mutilation of innocent men, then so be it. Success, after all, always had its price. And one didn't want to disappoint gods who had proved to be so generous.

As news of the gang's depraved activities became known, Police officials, anthropologists, and cult experts of every persuasion jumped on the bandwagon by attributing the bloody ways to one strange religion after another. But as the story continued developing, it became apparent that no single established religious faith was solely responsible, Constanzo had taken a sprinkle of this, a sprinkle of that, flavored the capricious mix with foul twists of his own demented design, and combined it all into a nauseating Faustian stew of religions.

The handsome youth, whom Mexicans called *El Cubano*, had started his own uniquely berserk, Manson-like belief system in his successful move to gain unquestioned control over the pathetically splintered gang of incompetent drug traffickers.

It was the human sacrifices that puzzled anthropologists and theologians the most. Animal sacrifice is common to a surprising number of religious cults around the world, but human ritual sacrifice was almost unheard of in modern Mexico. As a result, most experts agreed that the inventive Godfather borrowed more liberally from the African-Caribbean tradition than from Mexican folk religion — although he didn't ignore *Brujeria* completely.

After talking with suspected cult members about the gang's unholy activities, it became clear that *Santeria* played a prominent role in Constanzo's outrageous polyglot religion. *Santeria* is a sophisticated form of Cuban Voodoo with origins in the dark, mystical jungles of Africa, and a religion Constanzo was schooled in as a child in Puerto Rico and South Florida.

Santeria in its present form was first practiced around 2500 B.C. in what is now known as Nigeria, on the banks of the expansive Niger River. It was then that Yorba tribesmen first developed the nature religion that allowed mortals to approach the gods through worship of natural objects such as shells, feathers, and herbs.

Santeria — Spanish for "worship of saints" — spread to the New World in the 1500s when slavers brought captured black Africans to the Southern United States, and the Caribbean as an inexpensive source of manual labor.

The Africans had no choice but to work for their new masters, but they didn't really abandon their old gods. Ordered to adopt the white man's religion, many of them outwardly complied and, to their masters, seemed to have adopted Catholicism and its saints. But among themselves, the slaves learned to identify each of the saints with one of their own African gods. So when they were seen by owners apparently praying to a small clay image of Saint Lazarus, for instance, they may instead have been petitioning the ancient Yoruba god and patron of the sick, *Babalu-'Aye'*. Or if they were kneeling before an image of Christ on the cross, they may have been seeking communion with *Oloru'n-Orofi*, the Creator Himself.

The clandestine *Santeria* ceremonies helped homesick and frightened slaves maintain a strong bond with an Africa thousands of miles away. Gradually, the religion based on old Yoruba beliefs, with a strong meld of Catholicism, spread through the islands, Central and South America. The religion flourished in the New World, and although it maintained many of its secret ways, it gradually moved into the open; today it is widely practiced alongside Catholicism in the islands and in Latin America. *Santeria* established an especially strong foothold in Cuba and in Brazil, where, in slightly different form, it is known as *Macumba*, or *Umbanda*. And increasingly, worship of the old Yoruba gods has moved onto mainland North America and is growing in popularity among Hispanics, blacks, and Anglos.

Practitioners of *Santeria*, called *Santeros*, worship a bewildering array of deities, called *Orishas*, who are represented in their dual role as Catholic saints and ancient African gods. They can be summoned for help during times of need or crisis. *Santeros* maintain that the *orishas* are extremely powerful, and each controls specific aspects of life, such as purity, employment, health — and death.

A sampling of *orishas*, and the aspects they control, include *Agayu* (fatherhood), *Inle* (medicine), *Orula* (wisdom and destiny), *Oshun* (love) and *Yemaya* (maternity). Each *orisha* has a specific number, color, food, and emblem associated with it, as well as its personal Catholic saint and alter ego.

Santeria teaches that every person is assigned a specific *orisha* at birth as a sort of guardian angel, as well as a special plant, birthstone, and animal. If someone is able to discover his or her individual *orisha* while growing up, he can improve his chances of power and success in adulthood by always carrying with him his specific symbols.

An individual's lucky stone doesn't have to be a precious gem in the traditional sense. It can be something as simple as a pebble that draws your attention for no apparent reason, presumably because it is filled with good vibrations. You will recognize the stone should you be lucky enough to find it, *santeros* say, because you will feel an overwhelming need to own it and carry it with you. To do so ensures good luck.

Animals play an integral role in *Santeria*. Some are good, such as the goat, the elephant, and the turtle. Others are potentially bad, such as snakes, lizards, rats, and venomous insects. To attract good luck from a benevolent animal, believers must have its image in their home.

Water, too, is believed to have great protective power, and many *santeros* keep a small container beneath their beds specifically to protect them from evil spirits, which are captured and melt in water like a handful of spilled sugar. For best results, *santeros* believe, the water should be changed daily. Brown sugar and garlic are also considered to be powerful protective elements.

Santeria is based on the magic of gods. But unlike the Christian God, which is believed to be loving, generous and helpful to those who pray to Him and keep His law, the deities of *Santeria* must be appeased through tangible offerings to individual *orisha* and the aspect he or she controls.

Attracting a husband or wife, for example, would require the assistance of *Oshun,* who controls romantic love and marriage. To enlist her aid, believers must offer beads, honey, animal shells, a pumpkin or seashells. And if a candle is burned, it must be yellow, *Oshun*'s favorite color.

In a typical *Santeria* ceremony to bring back a lost lover, the supplicant hollows out a small pumpkin and places inside five claws from a rooster, an egg, some pepper, marjoram, Florida water, a slip of paper containing the name of the lost love and an article that person held close, such as some hair. The petitioner then spits inside the hollowed pumpkin and offers it to *Oshun,* leaving it in front of a statue of her alter-ego, Our Lady of Caridad del Cobre for nine days. On the tenth day the pumpkin is thrown into a river. If the spell is cast correctly, the lost love should return within five days.

Santeria's power is based on sympathetic magic, which adheres to the law of similarity. Like produces like, which is why magic performed on a specific person often involves a wax figure of that person. The individual performing the magic believes that whatever happens to the doll will also happen to the person, be it good or evil.

Another aspect of *Santeria*'s power is sometimes explained as "contagious magic," which is based on the belief that something which has had contact with someone will forever preserve that contact, no matter how distant they become. Consequently, *santeros* can work a spell on someone simply by using something they have been in contact with, such as a shirt, a few strands of hair, or even nail clippings.

Sacrificial offerings to *orishas* are necessary because they are considered living beings and therefore must eat to remain strong. Some objects selected for sacrifice to the hungry *orishas* are fairly innocuous, such as beads, honey or specific plants. But fresh animal blood is frequently required — an aspect that often appears inexplicably barbaric and grotesque to nonbelievers.

True *santeros* are convinced, however, that the blood sacrifice is necessary to prove the interdependence of living things and to give the *orishas* something in return for their helpful magic. Goats and chickens are the most common sacrificial animals, but *santeros* maintain that they are never treated cruelly. Their death is quick and without unnecessary pain, and the meat is almost always consumed by worshippers during ritual feasts, it is claimed.

It is the concept of animal sacrifice that has placed *Santeria* in such bad light. Many nonbelievers, especially those in metropolitan areas, still consider the practice to constitute animal cruelty and often call the police to inform about sacrificial rituals. The increasingly frequent discovery of the mutilated carcasses of goats and chickens in public parks, waterways, and abandoned tenements has also often been misinterpreted as the remains of some sort of Satanic ceremonies. It is not surprising then that most *santeros* choose to practice their religion quietly among themselves, and seldom share their secrets with outsiders.

By the time police discovered the heinous murders in Matamoros, *Santeria* had already come under attack in American cities with large Hispanic populations, including those in Miami, Chicago, and New York, because of its necessary blood offerings to the *orishas*. But defenders are quick to point out that *Santeria,* in its purist, modern form, has never called for human sacrifice — only the blood of animals. Human sacrifice is as foreign to *Santeria* as it is to modern-day Christianity, they insist.

Despite criticism from law enforcement agencies and animal rights activitists, *Santeria* continues to flourish, albeit quietly, throughout the United States, and *botanicas* — stores that sell icons and ritual items — can be found in almost any neighborhood with a heavy Cuban or Puerto Rican population.

Miami is an excellent example. With its burgeoning Cuban population, many settled in an area known as Little Havana, the rapidly growing South Florida metropolis is known to be home to more than 25,000 practicing *santeros*.

Most *santeros* eye outsiders with suspicion, and seldom detail their religious beliefs to nonbelievers. Their stonewall silence is understandable, considering the personal and public attacks that are increasingly being focused on their religion.

Nonbelievers seldom understand how the religion works and most have no apparent interest in learning, *santeros* bitterly complain. Outsiders are typically sidetracked by the intimidating blood sacrifices and seldom show any interest in digging deeper in an attempt to understand what is in reality as sophisticated a belief system as Christianity, Islam or Buddhism.

To *santeros,* the sacrifice of chickens and goats is as necessary and common as the Holy Communion is to Catholics. The ritual slaughter has even been compared by *Santeria*'s defenders to the religious rules for the preparation of kosher food for Jews.

"These sacrifices are our communion with the saints," explained a Cuban-born *Santeria* priest in Miami. "So why the constant persecution of *Santeria?*"

The slaughter of sacrificial animals has pitted *santeros* in south Florida against local government in a bitter dispute over freedom of religion. Florida statutes prohibiting cruelty to animals have been cited in efforts to stop the blood ceremonies. But *Santeros* have responded in court and in the press by insisting that the sacrifice of animals is their right as part of their religious sacraments.

In Hialeah, the Miami suburb where Constanzo spent much of his formative years, city officials banned the killing of animals except in designated slaughterhouses, after receiving a petition with 3,000 signatures asking that a downtown *Santeria* church be closed. The petition was circulated by a Hialeah attorney and vocal *Santeria* opponent, after the church opened down the street from his law office. In his complaint, he accused church members of involvement in animal cruelty because they slaughtered goats and fowl during religious ceremonies. Understandably, the ruling in Hialeah didn't set well with local *santeros*.

There was, however, Constitutional precedent for banning animal sacrifices. Although the Constitution guarantees freedom of belief, it says nothing about potentially dangerous or antisocial rituals. And over the years, snake-handling by fundamentalist Christians has been outlawed, along with the ritual smoking of marijuana by Ethiopian Coptics.

Miami's Dade county government has no laws that specifically deal with *Santeria* sacrifices, although zoning regulations effectively prohibit the slaughter of animals in single-family residential districts. Most police departments treat animal sacrifice complaints as animal cruelty calls.

Practitioners disagree with any label of animal cruelty or antisocial behavior. "It's worse to watch what happens in a boxing ring," one *santero* told a Miami newsman. "That is more cruel."

When the horror at the Santa Elena Ranch was uncovered, reporters were quick to point out the apparent connection between the ritual ceremonies of *Santeria* and the bloody Matamoros killer cult. But the link became even stronger when gang members told police that they were initiated into the religious ways of the cult through repeated viewings of the movie, *The Believers*.

Young Serafin Hernandez Garcia told authorities it was his favorite film.

There were startling similarities between Constanzo's gang and the evil cult portrayed in *The Believers*. Most significantly, both groups practiced human sacrifice to attain protection and power from the gods.

Practicing *santero* condemned the film when it was released in 1986, complaining loudly that viewers would confuse the movie's evil cult with *Santeria*, and erroneously assume that human sacrifice played a role in the relatively benign Afro-Caribbean religion. Their cries became louder when word was spread that Constanzo patterned his own unholy religious beliefs in part on the movie and used it to instill the proper spirit and respect in his followers.

Many video stores along the border said they could barely keep the film in stock once its cult connection was announced. "You'd think it was a new release, but it came out three years ago," said one dismayed video store employee. "I guess people are just genuinely interested and want to see what the movie's about, with all these killings going on."

Not all video stores joined in the bonanza, however. Once word was out, a leading Texas chain store removed *The Believers* from the shelves of their video section. Officials said the move was made because the company felt it wasn't right to profit from the nauseating slaughter in Matamoros. "We just don't want to buy into it," a corporate spokeswoman explained. "A tragedy occurred and let's just let it go."

Following news reports that linked the Matamoros gang with aspects of *Santeria,* prominent *santeros* flocked to the defense of their religion, noting that *Santeria* was no more to blame for the Matamoros horror than Christianity was to blame for the Jonestown massacre in Guyana.

Nevertheless, a darkly sinister side of the religious belief brought to the West by African slaves persists in cropping up. Rogue *santeros* — or practitioners of closely related beliefs — have repeatedly been linked to grave robbing as they search for skulls and other bones and human body parts for rituals. And many of the criminals who arrived in the U.S. during the Mariel boat-lift from Cuba in 1980 practice negative forms of the religion. Judges and police have been threatened and cursed with spells, and mutilated carcasses of animals have been left at entrances of public buildings and on doorsteps of private homes all over the country, after being butchered in dread rituals.

There have been *Santeria* murders, as well. In Miami retired welterweight boxing title contender Jose Stable was sentenced to life in prison for the shooting death of a policeman attempting to take him to court. Stable had split a coconut in a *Santeria* ritual and observed what he believed to be occult signs indicating he should not surrender. Based on those signs, Stable killed the policeman who tried to take him away.

And a few years ago in New York, a young Puerto Rican boy was ritually murdered and left hanging upside down inside an abandoned tenement. His body had been drained of blood during a debauched rite designed to appease thirsty gods, police said.

There were also indications that Constanzo's followers incorporated aspects of an ominous religion called *Palo Mayombe* into their bloody rites. Described by experts as an evil black-magic flip side of *Santeria, Palo Mayombe* is a religion whose disciples call for help from Catholic saints, ancient African spirit gods and the tortured souls of the enslaved dead. It has its roots in the impenetrable jungles of the African Congo, and like *Santeria,* its practice was melded with Catholicism by slaves after reaching the New World.

Some *santeros* keep two altars in their homes — one for *Santeria* and one for *Palo Mayombe.* Their approach to natural magic is similar, but there are vast differences between the two beliefs. *Santeria* reputedly offers its gods the

HELL RANCH

blood of animal sacrifices killed quickly and humanely, while the animal and human sacrifices offered during some *Palo Mayombe* rituals are deliberately tortured and horribly mutilated. Pain and fear are powerful elements of the rites.

Sometimes the blood of the sacrificial victim is consumed by participants in ceremonies, acts occasionally followed by other vile forms of necrophilia and cannibalism. Parts of victims are boiled in black *n'gangas* — similar to the crimson-tinged cauldrons found in the ceremonial hut on the Santa Elena Ranch. *Palo Mayombe* cultists believe that the spirits of the victims will become trapped in the cauldrons and enslaved, to be called on for protection or to carry out evil. Some *Palo Mayombe* practitioners prefer that brain tissue be left in skulls used in the obscene acts of necromancy so that the agonized spirits they have summoned can think and act more intelligently.

A heavy dash of *Palo Mayombe* fits perfectly into the plans of many drug-running cults like Constanzo's, experts have pointed out, because mixing drugs with black magic creates an organization that is even more loyal and willing to do whatever the cult leader says. For many such groups, moving drugs can become a spiritual act, not just a business.

Fortunately, *Palo Mayombe* is nowhere near as prevalent as *Santeria* in the U.S. and Latin America. And even among those who do practice the loathsome African religion, it is believed that most obtain body parts necessary to their vulgar rituals by robbing graves or from medical supply warehouses — not through human sacrifice. Under Constanzo's leadership, the Matamoros-Mexico City drug smuggling gang appears to have taken the necrophilic religion back to its deepest African roots by killing, mutilating, and dismembering fresh sacrifices — healthy young men chosen specifically for that purpose.

One respected cultural anthropologist told journalists that practitioners of *Palo Mayombe* use human bones and other body parts because it gives them a sense of security.

"They believe they control the spirits that were once in those bodies. To them it's like having a slave," explained Rafael Martinez of Miami. "People turn to this magical practice of *n'ganga* in times of stress and it gives them a solution. Drug trafficking brings a lot of insecurity and *n'ganga* gives the practitioners a sense of control."

When police officials began interrogating members of Constanzo's gang rounded up at the Santa Elena Ranch, they were confused about the murderous cult's specific religious practices. *Santeria* was initially suspect, especially after Serafin Hernandez Garcia, Jr., advised them that *The Believers* was his favorite film. Elio Hernandez Rivera, however, helped clear up the confusion when he said that *Santeria* had played only a minor role in the cult's religious beliefs, and that its spiritual doctrine revolved more around *Palo Mayombe*.

"Elio made Serafin a *Palo Mayombe* priest," Lieutenant Gavito told reporters. "But Serafin didn't really know what it was he was practicing because all he had on his mind was that movie."

Practitioners of *Santeria* and *Palo Mayombe* say their religion is benign, but not everyone accepts that. The attorney who crossed swords with *santeros* in Hialeah says that *Palo Mayombe* and *Santeria* are one and the same. "It attracts the worst elements of society and it's based primarily on fear. The priests are paid money to put curses on people," he told newsmen.

The Mexican folk belief, *Brujeria,* dates back to the time of the ancient Aztecs, and was also part of Constanzo's bastard religious practice. As he was growing up, Constanzo understood the amazing power his claims of healing abilities, clairvoyance and spell-casting talents could have over people, especially in superstitious Mexico. So it seemed only natural that *Brujeria* would play an important role in the religious mishmash he fashioned for his drug-running cultists.

Brujeria is important and respected in Mexico, where folk beliefs have been relied on in times of need for centuries. Before Christianity was introduced to the Indians by zealous Spanish priests, the primary deity of Old World *Brujeria* was the ancient Aztec Goddess Tonantzin. She was an all-powerful, benevolent goddess who watched over her people and cared for them. Tonantzin, under the name Tlazolteotl, also purged believers of sin through regular confessions to her priests and priestesses, witches or shamans who held secret rituals to benefit all who believed in them.

However, an Aztec goddess, no matter how loving, didn't set very well with the missionary priests, who accompanied the *conquistadores* seeking new souls for Christ. They couldn't wipe out worship of the goddess, so they gave her a new Christian identity. She became Our Lady of Guadalupe. The Indians obediently accepted the convenient name change, but deep down they still considered her the same old Goddess. *Brujeria* is still strong in Mexico, because it has continued to change with the times and with the people.

Indeed, *Brujeria* is as popular today in the hearts and minds of the Mexican people as it was hundreds of years ago when Catholic missionaries were converting the Indians to Christian ways. *Brujeria* is a religion of the lowliest farmer and the most successful business man, and Guadelupe oversees all who believe in her, caring for them in times of need and giving them hope when the future is bleak. The Lady is so revered that she is the Patron saint of Mexico.

Native people reluctant to fully renounce their old gods and beliefs melded *Brujeria* with Catholicism, the strong, demanding religion newly introduced from Europe, as others had done with the religions of the Yoruba and the people of the Congo. And there were already certain similarities between the religious doctrines of Catholicism and *Brujeria.*

Followers of the goddess Tonantzin believed that all the stars and planets were her children. The Indians perceived a close resemblance to the children of Tonantzin and the saints and angels in heaven that make up the Catholic pantheon of higher spiritual beings. The ancient Aztec form of *Brujeria* also maintained that when a person died, the soul went to Mictlan, an unpleasant place that looked suspiciously like Catholicism's purgatory. There was a form of Hell, as well, that was ruled by the Lord of the Dead, a deity known as Mictlantecuhtli. Christians know him as Satan.

Brujas, the traditional folk witches who cast spells and heal illness, are still a major part of *Brujeria* in Mexico and Chicano communities in the United States. Over the past few years they have received a renewed respect by researchers who realize they serve a real and needed service among believers. Many modern doctors and therapists who work closely with a primarily Mexican population, in fact, have *brujas* on staff to comfort clients and aid in the healing process.

Magic and witchcraft play a vital role in *Brujeria*. Spells and hexes are a real part of the religion's power and appeal, and considerable energy is spent by believers seeking the casting of spells, or their removal.

A significant amount of time is also spent by *brujas* and *brujos* praying to The Lady of Guadalupe for help in righting perceived wrongs or teaching someone a lesson. One well-known *Brujeria* legend recounts the tale of a lecherous old man who made the mistake of attempting to press his affections on a decorous and proper *bruja*. Outraged, she demanded an apology, but the old man refused. He made matters worse by insulting her appearance and reputation. That night the *bruja* got her revenge by praying to The Lady of Guadalupe, who punished the old man and his entire family by turning them into goats.

The retributive justice dished out by The Lady of Guadalupe and her *brujas* on the Earthly plane of existence is one thing. The curse issued by a *diablesa,* a bad witch, is something else. Most believers in *Brujeria* assume that punishment meted out by The Lady of Guadalupe is deserved, but bad witches supposedly have been known to hex even the innocent. And their detestable spells must be fought with every means available. Usually this means enlisting the aid of a powerful *bruja*, who can call down the all-mighty power of The Lady of Guadalupe to remove the hex and punish the *diablesa* who issued it.

Brujos and *curanderos* are commonly called upon during times of illness. The shamanic healers rely on ritual prayers to The Lady of Guadalupe and a unique and potent knowledge of native herbalism to heal diseases of the body and the mind. The herbal aspect makes perfect sense, since modern medicine acknowledges the healing aspects of many types of plants and trees. But during some *Brujeria* healing rituals, the herbs appear to take second place to the incredible healing power of the mind. Prayer and faith are powerful healers, and sometimes they can do more good than the strongest medicine. During the long history of *Brujeria* in Mexico, there are legends of *curanderos* curing terminal cancer and even mending broken bones using arcane combinations of prayer and herbs. The stories, which are widely repeated, help maintain *Brujeria*'s influence and spread its popularity among believers.

Faith healing is a common aspect of *Brujeria*, and many believers rely on it implicity to help them overcome disease or remain healthy. Mexico is overpopulated with the poor, and for some, faith healing provided by the local *curandero* is the only medical care they can afford.

The *curandero*'s approach to medicine is often unique to the individual. Some place themselves in a hypnotic trance to diagnose the patient, then rely on a vast array of dried herbs and healing potions to cure the problem. Faith in The Lady of Guadalupe plays a strong role in cases such as these, but medicinal plants alone are often sufficiently effective.

Other *curanderos* hypnotize patients and question them to locate the pain, then turn to herbal remedies and a healing touch.

For many Mexicans, life without regular consultations with a *curandero* or *brujo* is inconceivable. The witches and healers are considered seers, and many believers seek their wisdom before making the most important and the most mundane decisions.

Seers skilled in the clairvoyant arts of *Brujeria* call on a glittering grab-bag of shamanic techniques to foretell the future. Some consult a form of tarot, others read globs of hot wax dropped in cold water, the entrails or droppings of fowl and other small animals, to bizarre talismans. Still others rely on magnets and the clients "magnetic polarity." The ways of foretelling the future are many. So are the questions seers are commonly asked. Housewives consult their personal *brujo* in matters of romance, pregnancy, childbearing, and domestic relationships. Some successful businessmen with respectable positions in major corporations wouldn't consider starting the day without seeking the advice of their favorite seer on the best time to travel, close a deal, or play the stockmarket.

Belief in *Brujeria, Santeria, Palo Mayombe* and Voodoo is so strong in Mexico and in some parts of the United States that *botanicas* and other stores catering to the followers of the religions can be found in nearly every sizable neighborhood. In some cities with large Hispanic populations, such as Miami, Houston, Los Angeles, and Chicago, there are neighborhoods where *bontanicas* can be found two or three to a block.

The stores cater to superstition and carry almost everything needed to cast a spell, remove a hex or heal a physical or mental disorder. Shelves are piled high with Haitian Voodoo dolls, wooden crucifixes, protective amulets, medicinal herbs, fragrant incense, and colorful votive candles to summon or give thanks to the deity of your choice. They also carry statues of Catholic saints for practitioners of *Santeria, Palo Mayombe, Brujereia* — or *Macumba, Umbanda, Candomble,* and Voodoo-like cults popular in Brazil.

Books advising how to cast spells, and how to remove them, are stocked in many of the stores. Most popular in many areas of the country, however, are special decorative glass containers with candles inside. The images on the glass can be of anyone from St. Francis to Mexican revolutionary and bandit Pancho Villa. The candles are burned on home altars during private religious rituals.

Constanzo knew better than anyone the incredible power of *Brujeria,* and he used it freely to control his gang and superstitious associates involved in the transportation of marijuana and other drugs across the Mexican-U.S. border. The degree of influence of an acknowledged *brujo* such as Constanzo ultimately depends on a combination of fear and power, and *El Padrino* used both to unify the Hernandez and Mexico City gangs and keep the organization strong. Experts on religious cults understood Constanzo's abilities well. Like the priests of the ancient Aztecs, Constanzo repeatedly proved himself to be a man of power and not to be trifled with. His followers believed that not only was his own power immense, but he also held the avaricious power of gods who glutted on human blood.

The final component of Constanzo's weird religious pastiche was a healthy dose of *Santismo.* Based on vivid fantasies about the ancient warrior strength and magic of the Aztecs, *Santismo* practices call for the hacking out of human organs as sacrificial offerings to the divinities. Constanzo performed the mutilation with obscene pleasure. It was always an awesomely degenerate spectacle that captured the hearts and minds of his servile sycophants with arcane incantations, prayer, the vivid use of imagery and raw horror. Witnesses to Constanzo's insane performances before the bloodstained altar on the Santa Elena Ranch were entranced by his charisma and animal energy. He was a man destined to lead through murder, mayhem, and magic.

Police officials and journalists were eager to find a simple label that would explain the monstrous behavior at the Hell Ranch. The Press avidly researched, interviewed and explained the strange Pandora's box of religions. Anthropologists, theologists, criminologists, and experts in cults were consulted for information and titillating quotes.

The flood of negative publicity that vomited from Matamoros, focusing first on one exotic cult, then another, further agitated and alarmed an already skittish public. And it worried innocent devotees of *Santeria, Brujeria,* and other belief systems caught up in the hysterics and commonly branded in the public mind as devil worship, or Satanism. Even organized Satanists issued public statements disavowing themselves of any connection to the degenerate drug smuggling cultists.

Adherents of *Santeria, Palo Mayombe,* Voodoo, *Wicca* and *Brujeria,* all vehemently denied any connection with the heinous crimes at the Santa Elena Ranch. Constanzo was a rogue who stole bits and pieces from various cult denominations and used them for his own demented purposes, they declared. He was not a practicing member of any recognized religion.

The leaders of some of the nation's larger *Santeria* churches reinforced their earlier claims that news reports were offering a twisted and unfair portrayal of their faith.

"It's guilt by association," complained Ernesto Pichardo, a *Santeria* priest in the Church of the Lukumi Babalu Aye in Hialeah, where Constanzo lived before moving to Mexico City. "It will possibly force us to very quickly respond to negative publicity with some sort of public education in order to reduce that kind of (prejudiced) reaction."

Pichardo went on to blame an irresponsible press for scaring an already frightened population with unfounded tales of religious terror. Unfortunately, he said, those who would suffer the most were the *Santeria* religion and the innocent people who believe in it.

The label of "Voodoo" is usually placed on any religious belief that is inherently different from Christianity, Judaism, or Islam — especially if it involves so-called African rituals such as drumming and dancing, or the sacrifice of animals, he observed.

True Voodoo — or *Vodun* — is a popular Haitian nature religion brought to the west by slaves from what is now known as the Republic of Benin. Like *Santeria,* it involves a number of deities who protect and care for believers in return for sacrificial offerings.

Sandoval said that the problem arises when the religion is embraced as a coping mechanism, and some people may use it for evil purposes. Any magical or ritual practice will attract people on the fringes of society, she stated. Unfortunately, African religions usually get the most attention.

The tragedy in Matamoros sparked renewed interest in the threat of Satanic cult activity in the United States, even though Constanzo's group apparently didn't practice Satanism.

Evidence of Satanic violence has been growing alarmingly throughout the U.S. Desecration of cemeteries and the robbing of human remains by people believed to be involved in self-styled Satanic rituals has been reported in virtually every state. And Satanic graffiti is common in areas where teenagers congregate.

California appears to be particularly troubled by neo-Satanists, and parents are concerned — especially following the brouhaha resulting from the Matamoros cult slayings and a rash of family murders by young disciples of the Prince of Darkness. The slaughter in Matamoros was shocking, but some experts believe there may be a positive fallout because it has attracted the attention of some people who previously refused to believe in the threat of blood cults.

"As awful as the murders in Mexico were, maybe people here will finally open their eyes," Peggy Smith, vice president of the Sonoma County, California-based Victims of Systems, told reporters. "There's a long history of cults in this area, and it's time something was done about it."

California residents have been staggered by reports of Satanic activity. In Ukiah, three teenagers, who belonged to a group called "Children of Death," casually strolled into a branch of the county health department and asked if it was possible to get AIDS by drinking blood. Until then, the youngsters, mostly high school students who liked to parade around in white-face and black clothing, had attracted little attention. But their bizarre query suddenly cast them in a different light. Just what were they up to?, alarmed townspeople began to ask themselves. Some of their fellow students said the "Children of Death" bragged that they were members of a Satanic cult.

In nearby Sonoma County, residents were shocked by a string of dead cats that were found over a two-year period skinned and drained of blood. The animals' hearts were ripped out.

The skinned cats found throughout Sonoma County are still a mystery, but the ritual killing of animals is nothing new to the area. In 1985, the bodies of twenty-five decapitated goats were discovered. "People thought they had just been slaughtered," a field supervisor with the Sonoma County Humane society warned. "Today, we have to look at it differently. People are looking at this stuff too lightly. They don't want to believe it's going on, but it's here and we'd better try to stop it."

Many clergymen used the murders in Matamoros as a springboard to warn parents of the influence of satanic cults. Often preaching with classic fire and brimstone, the clergymen talked about how to protect loved ones and how to tell if children are involved in satanic groups. In extreme cases, experts told enthralled audiences, young people may be into self-mutilation, aggressive behavior and an obsessive fascination with blood and death.

In Texas, it was revealed following the Matamoros slayings that cult-related activity was up, and most of it centered in the southern half of the state.

According to the State Department of Public Safety, which acts as a cult clearinghouse, more than 225 cases of possible cult activity were reported between 1985 and 1989.

The reported incidents ranged from mere suspicion of cult activity involving young people, to the actual discovery of altars or ceremonial cauldrons at locations searched by law enforcement officers, most of whom are now better trained to detect such activity.

Robert Urbanek, a cult expert and detective with the San Antonio Police Department, reported that evidence of rituals has been found in cemeteries, vacant houses and farms. "Some of it's Satanism and some of it's *Santeria*," he told news reporters. "Is it bigger here? No bigger than in Dallas or Kansas City. This kind of things is everywhere."

One of the biggest attractions to cult activity among young people, Texas officials warned, was the prevalence of illegal drugs, including hallucinogens and marijuana. Hallucinogenic drugs, including LSD and psychedelic mushrooms, are often used to heighten the senses during Satanic ceremonies.

Most so-called cult activity is relatively harmless, but sometimes the dark side makes an ugly appearance. In one well-publicized case in December 1988, a young Hispanic was found dead near a dirt road in Hutchins, Texas. The youth's eyelids had been cut off and two pennies were found on the road near his head. The case is still unsolved, but authorities believe the boy was the victim of a drug-related ritual killing performed by a member of a black magic cult.

Adolfo de Jesus Constanzo used religion to further his own twisted goals, but in the end he was betrayed by the same gods for whom he murdered. The protection they were supposed to provide never materialized, and his carefully assembled and indoctrinated gang was arrested and his lucrative drug business was destroyed. Just like the movies, good triumphed over evil. But the toll in human lives, suffering and fear was high, and it would be a long time before the terrifying shockwaves set in motion before his evil empire collapsed would begin to fade.

CHAPTER 11

Jitters

THE SHOCK WAVES GENERATED by the ghoulish discovery in Matamoros on April 11, 1989, flashed like lightning through the Rio Grande Valley and around the world.

Matamoros and Brownsville, two seemingly tiny and insignificant dots on the map, had instantly become household names. Everyone in the Valley was talking about the shocking murders and the bloodthirsty cultists. And the talk could only mean misery for the reputation and economy of the border communities.

Businessmen and civic leaders in both Brownsville and Matamoros worried about the devastating impact of the murders that was almost certain to descend on local tourism.

An ugly stench of violent death had enveloped the border like a Biblical plague. Tourists were no longer fretting over the heat; they were afraid for their lives.

One of the most troubling elements of the conundrum they found themselves in was the fact that the leaders of the murderous cult were still at large. That alone was enough to ensure that skittish tourists would be packing their suitcases and heading for safer surroundings far from the border. Merchants who depended on the tourist trade were already moaning, in fact, about dwindling revenues, and empty stores, bars and restaurants.

Hoping to lure back some of the wary North Americans with dollars to spend, the Matamoros Chamber of Commerce aired a series of positive radio and television spots. If the advertising campaign helped any, there were few who noticed. North Americans were afraid to go to Matamoros while leaders of the mad killer cultists might still be roaming the streets searching for new victims.

The loss of tourists was rapidly reflected in a startling increase in the flow of illegal immigrants across the border. Barely two months after the horror was uncovered at the Hell Ranch, a border patrol official in Laredo, Texas, confirmed that tourism had dropped by forty to forty-five percent in the Nuevo Laredo area, radically hiking unemployment and encouraging

Mexicans in border cities to cross the Rio Grande and look for work in the north.

But discovery of the death ranch had an equally chilling effect on the locals. Matamoros and Brownsville are filled with residents who firmly believe in eerie occult powers, in evil witches, devils, the evil eye and deadly curses that can cripple or kill. And the heinous cult murders at the Santa Elena Ranch affected them like few other crimes ever could. It was supernatural evil at its very worst, and they were stalked by fears that the devil's work might yet be unfinished. The fears became paranoia.

Anonymous telephone calls were made in Brownsville and Matamoros, warning that cultists were going to begin kidnapping schoolchildren as revenge for the arrests at the ranch. One of the callers, a woman who telephoned a radio station in Matamoros, identified herself as Sara Maria Aldrete Villarreal and threatened to kidnap forty school children as hostages. She said they would be burned alive if the suspected cultists arrested at the ranch were not freed. The fears were fueled by police reports disclosing that the blood-stained clothing of children had been found in her room in Matamoros, and suspicions that some of the victims were youngsters.

The threat was not from *La Padrina,* and the calls were nothing more than a cruel and stupid hoax. But parents panicked. Despite the soothing assurances of police and school officials, and the posting of guards around campuses, hundreds of frightened children were pulled from their classrooms by panicky parents. And many of those who let their children continue their studies refused to allow them to travel to and from school unattended. The parents were scared to death of the cultists, whom Mexican newspapers had labeled as *narcosatanicos.*

Feeding on the fear that covered the region, unrelated rumors of satanic kidnapping flashed through three rural East Texas schools the same day, causing jittery parents to pull nearly 400 students from classrooms, despite reassurances from school district officials that the stories were nothing more than a vicious hoax.

Officials traced the rumors to Hemphill, a flyspeck town of 2,000, where an anxious mother reportedly received a call from her mother-in-law warning of schoolyard kidnappings. The story quickly spread, and panic wasn't far behind.

According to school district officials, the entire incident apparently started when mischievous students, pretending to be school administrators, telephoned a few parents and told them to come and take their children home. Teachers were amazed at how easily the parents were taken in by the panic, and loudly insisted that school is one of the safest places a child can be because they receive constant supervision.

Some police speculate that the fears of residents in the small Texas town were fueled both by the recent murders in Matamoros and by the brutal slaying of a woman in nearby Newton County a month earlier. In that bizarre case, a fourteen-year-old boy reputedly killed his thirty-two-year-old mother after entering into a Satanic death pact with a friend.

In the Valley town of Pharr, cult paranoia manifested itself in a different way when the Bible-based Church of Fire mysteriously burned to the ground. Rumors quickly started that the church had been used for Satanic rituals and was set afire as revenge for the cult murders in Matamoros. However, no evidence of anything suspicious was found at the charred ruins of the church, which had served the community for sixteen years, and fire officials blamed the blaze on faulty wiring.

Nonetheless, parents in the small rural community were frightened by subsequent rumors of cult kidnappings, police said, and many pulled their children from classes just to be safe. The Pharr-San Juan-Alamo School District immediately posted guards and demanded that police investigate the rumors.

Tabloid talk shows, recognizing a great opportunity, jumped on the story with a vengeance. Talk show hosts Oprah Winfrey, and Geraldo Rivera — who scored big in the ratings with a previous prime time special on the threat of Satanism in the United States — went head to head on the story, releasing very similar shows only a few days apart.

Geraldo, aided in Brownsville by co-host Bob Salter from KSAT-TV in San Antonio, spent an hour grilling people close to the case for information, his focus always on the most gruesome details of the ritual deaths performed by the cult and on the fear and panic that permeated the region. On the panel were Cameron County Sheriff's Lieutenant George Gavito, a stern-faced, plain-talking cop's cop, who wears a white ten-gallon hat and cowboy boots; Texas Southmost College anthropology professor Tony Zavaleta; and Texas Attorney General Jim Mattox, all of whom struggled to keep the show sane, thoughtful, and informative.

Rivera was out for ratings, however, and wasted no time in describing in the goriest, most gut-churning detail, the horrible manner in which the cultists' victims were killed and dismembered.

Horrified Brownsville city officials quickly responded with bitter criticism of the aggressive talk show host for dwelling on the most morbid cultist aspects of the ritual slayings, and all but ignoring the fact that the gang members were, above anything else, drug smugglers.

Zavaleta, who is a Brownsville city commissioner as well as an instructor at TSC, accused Rivera of dragging the town "into his dog and pony show," and Mayor Ygnacio Garza angrily labelled the show — titled "Drugs, Death and the Devil" — a waste of time. Government officials were especially upset during the taping because Mattox repeatedly had to correct statements referring to Brownsville as the killing site.

A spokeswoman for Rivera responded with a spirited defense of the popular, although widely criticized, NBC tabloid TV show host. Reading from a prepared statement, she told the press: "I am not going to apologize about a program on one of the most sensationalistic Satanic tragedies in American history coming off on the sensationalistic side.

"It's not unusual for participants on a 'Geraldo Show' to want to act like producers. That's understandable. But we attempted to cover as many aspects of this barbaric crime as we could within the confines of only one hour of TV time."

Oprah Winfrey was close behind Geraldo with her own coverage of the Matamoros tragedy, inviting Mark Kilroy's pal Bill Huddleston, Bill's mother Gwen, and Mattox onto the TV studio stage. The Kilroys were also invited on the show, but declined, apologizing that it was too soon after Mark's murder to talk about their tragedy on television.

The horror of the Matamoros killings also prompted a Houston radio station to drop a recently initiated and heavily promoted morning gag skit called "Voodoo Wednesday." Station officials on KZFX-FM shelved the program indefinitely, saying it was insensitive and could be construed as making light of the tragedy.

The ill-timed Voodoo skit offered listeners an opportunity to phone the station and jokingly put a curse on a spouse, lover, boss, salesman or anyone else giving them trouble. The real-life Voodoo tragedy that struck the suburban Houston family of Mark Kilroy took the intended humor out of the skit.

"We certainly don't want our image as being in favor of Voodoo," a station spokesman explained to the press. "We have sympathy with the Kilroy family."

At Texas Southmost College, a student-sponsored three-day lecture series on Satanism and the occult — which was planned long before the discovery of the cult murders in Matamoros — drew a mob of people anxious to learn more about the cult murder horror. Speakers included a former Satanic high priest and an El Paso clergyman, who was said to have survived occult rituals and brainwashing as a child. The timing of the Christian-oriented anti-cult lecture series was described by a school spokesman as no more than "a scary coincidence."

The owner of a private dance school in Brownsville organized a nondenominational outdoor prayer service outside her studios that drew about one hundred people, who joined hands to ask for divine assistance to cope with the tragedy. They prayed for the victims, survivors, investigators, and everyone in the shaken community.

Help for the families of the cult's victims quickly became a priority matter in the Matamoros-Brownsville area, and Mattox proposed extending the use of the Texas Crime Victims Compensation Fund to aid people who are victims of crime in a foreign country.

The proposal stemmed from the fact that although Mark Kilroy's parents spent thousands of dollars searching for their son, they were ineligible for crime victim's assistance because he was abducted and murdered in Mexico.

An outpouring of public concern for the Kilroys led to the establishment of a private fund on their behalf. And a San Antonio funeral home even offered to pay to have Mark's remains shipped back to Santa Fe for burial. The president of the funeral home said he felt an obligation to the Kilroys to see that they were properly represented during such a tragic time in their lives.

In the wake of the ritual murders, Texas State Senator Judith Zaffirini also proposed a bill that would provide even tougher penalties against individuals who abuse or kill a child under sixteen during a Satanic ritual. "I believe that the penalty should be higher because the penalty would fit the crime," she said.

The legislator explained that the goal of the bill would be to deter the abuse of children and young teenagers as part of cult-related rituals.

Not all of her colleagues on the senate agreed with the measure, however. Senator Craig Washington objected to the proposal, complaining that it would only make the Penal Code even more confusing, especially for lawyers who already had trouble enough keeping up with the changes in the system. The measure nonetheless appeared to strike a sympathetic cord among a populace worried that such crimes could become even more common.

Residents of the Rio Grande Valley were suddenly inundated with news coverage of an ugly and unwanted incident in the life of their community as journalists descended on Matamoros. Parents found themselves faced with the unpleasant task of discussing with their children subjects they considered revolting. There was spirited debated among psychologists and other specialists in behavioral science about whether or not it was best to examine the problem with children — and frightened adults — or to down play its emotional impact.

A history professor at Homer Hanna High School in Brownsville encouraged parents and teachers to talk about the tragedy and to bring it into focus with objective information instead of focusing on grisly horror stories.

Child psychologists agreed with the assessment, noting that children respond well to frightening situations when their parents listen and show they care — even if they don't have all the answers. Honest information about cult activity could also provide valuable information to help vulnerable children resist being drawn into Satanic cult activity, the experts added.

Satanic worship is a pervasive problem throughout the Rio Grande Valley, a child psychologist warned. If a child is feeling depressed or rejected, he or she may feel isolated and begin to gravitate toward it.

As news of the Matamoros cult continued to spread, the media, looking for an easy label, continually referred to Sara Aldrete as a "witch" — an association that didn't set well with "good" witches across the U.S.

Most North American witches trace their spiritual ancestry to the pre-Christian paganism of western Europe. Although organized WICCA is split into denominations, much as Protestant Christianity, with its Lutherans, Episcopalians, Methodists, and Baptists, most agree that it is a benign nature religion, with a broad pantheon of gods. They do not sacrifice animals or humans, and although they still differ over whether or not homosexuals have a place in a fertility religion and whether or not the Mother Goddess is superior to the Horned God, their rituals are generally conducted with love and healing in mind. They do not even recognize a god sharing the evil aspects of the Judeo-Christian deity, Satan.

Laurie Cabot, who was appointed by Governor Michael Dukakis as the "official witch" of Salem, Massachusetts in 1975, started a letter-writing campaign to protest the label and to argue that associating witchcraft with the gruesome ritual killings in Mexico was a violation of the civil rights of witches everywhere. "We are not Satanists; we do not do black magic or any evil magic," said the Massachusetts activist, who formed the 900-member Witches League for Self-Awareness in 1986.

"We are trying to raise the consciousness of these people so we are not harmed. We need to separate ourselves from this hateful propaganda."

On the Mexican side of the border, civic and religious leaders were heartsick and angered at the tragedy, and at the likely effect of the flood of negative publicity on the economic and spiritual life of residents. A Matamoros school official cautioned that it wasn't fair to blame the entire community for the outrageous actions of a few people.

Comandante Benitez Ayala blamed irresponsible reports in the media for spreading irrational fears. He especially criticized Mexican newspapers for practicing yellow journalism by circulating reports that the *Padrina* had threatened to kidnap school children. "This is bogus. There was no truth to that story," he said.

Church leaders on both sides of the border noticed a surge in attendance at services, communion, and confessions. Father Ruperto Ayala Espinosa, a priest at Our Lady of Refuge, the Catholic cathedral that dominates the main Plaza in Matamoros, was quoted in the American Press as observing that after the dreadful discoveries at the Santa Elena Ranch, people were admitting to themselves that, "yes, evil exists."

One high-ranking Matamoros official declared: "The massacre of thirteen people at Santa Elena Ranch does not diminish any city in particular — it diminishes the human being." He talked of the black mark the crimes had left on the city, of parents who were afraid to let their children play in the street, and of the need not to panic.

"The death penalty is not enough for the people responsible for the killings at the Santa Elena Ranch. Because of the diabolical manner in which the killings were done, I am in favor of the death sentence. Not even with this, though, will they pay."

In Reynosa, a few miles west of Matamoros, Monsignor Carlos Vega Perez castigated increased liberalism. "When a human has a lot of freedom and it isn't used in the service of God, then you will look for the protection and service of the devil," he declared.

A Methodist clergyman in Rio Bravo, between Matamoros and Reynosa, warned that pop music, art, even television commercials, have the devil in them. But there was no cause for fear, because God is more powerful than the devil.

The cult murders were the hottest topic of discussion in Mexico until the strongest earthquake to rock Mexico City since the killer quake of 1985, struck on April 25 — adding more fear and panic to a nation that had already experienced more than its share.

The tremor registered 6.8 on the Richter scale, and although the epicenter was forty miles east of Acapulco, the shock waves were powerful enough to destroy several buildings two hundred miles away in Mexico City and send hundreds to hospitals. Surprisingly, there was only one death blamed on the quake.

Nonetheless, the tremor caused panic among residents in the capital city who vividly remembered the thousands killed in 1985. For a city already gripped by fear and Satanic paranoia, the quake could not have come at a worse time.

As Mexican and American law enforcement agencies concentrated on finding the fugitive outlaws responsible for the murder and mutilation on the Santa Elena Ranch, the victims of the ritual slayings were taken to two Matamoros funeral homes for identification and burial.

More than sixty people from throughout Mexico and the Rio Grande Valley region made the mournful journey to the funeral homes. Some traveled long distances. One old woman dressed in black came from the southern city of Loma Bonita, Oaxaca — more than 1,000 miles away — to view the remains, looking for her missing son. A negative identification meant renewed hope that a loved one was still alive, while a positive identification at least answered some of the many questions that had been plaguing survivors.

Tears of grief and expressions of horror and disbelief were common in the El Rosario and Glayosso funeral homes as family after family shuffled in for a glance at the pitiful remains. Some were little more than bones, a bit of rotting flesh and rags of clothes. Nevertheless, anxious,sad-faced relatives of long-missing men fearfully scanned the bodies for a recognizable face, a familiar piece of clothing or telltale marks.

The mother and sister of a handsome thirty-two-year-old Houston welder shared in the grim ordeal. He had been missing for a year,since travelling across the International Bridge for a night on the town in Matamoros. Then he vanished, suddenly dropping from sight, and thus becoming one of about one hundred men and women who were reported missing in Matamoros in the year before Mark Kilroy's abduction. The welder's mother and sister didn't identify any of the bodies at the two funeral homes as his, but others did find relatives among the newly butchered.

Anguished family members identified Ernesto Rivas Dias, the welder from Monterrey, Neuvo Leon, by the red cross he had tattooed on his left hand.

A red rose tattoo led to the identification of Matamoros Police Officer Jorge Valente del Fierro Gomez. The telltale mark was on the thirty-five-year-old lawman's right arm.

Tomas Garza Hernandez recognized her thirty-year-old son, Ruben Vela Garza, by his thick, black beard. He had been a farm worker on a ranch near the small Mexican border community of La Pesca. He was a quiet man with only a few years of schooling. He hadn't been seen by friends or family since the middle of February. He was last remembered by relatives, being hustled into a rusty Suburban with Florida license plates. After making the identification, Vela Garza's heartbroken mother lurched from the funeral home, clutching a wrinkled handkerchief to her mouth, her eyes swimming with tears as she wailed in Spanish, "It can't be. It can't be."

Some relatives couldn't handle the anticipated horror of viewing the remains directly, and pleaded to look at photographs instead. It was easier that way, they said.

Twenty-seven-year-old Esguiel Rodriguez Luna, a Matamoros farm worker, and another man who had led a double life, was recognized as one of the victims as shaken relatives inspected photographs.

Five of the more mutilated and decomposed bodies were buried in a pauper's cemetery before they could be positively identified, because in Mexico, state law requires funeral homes to hold remains for no longer than sixty-two hours. The bodies also posed a health threat because of their advanced state of decomposition. Photographs were taken of the bodies for future reference, but for some families, confirmation of the fate of loved ones would probably never be forthcoming.

The particularly violent method of death and mutilation made identification of the bodies difficult. Police revealed that although one victim was apparently burned, and another one or two shot to death, most were hacked and stabbed to death with machetes and knives. The brains, hearts, and lungs were viciously ripped from the bodies of those who died as human sacrifices in the demonic rituals. Several had their spines ripped from their rotting bodies after burial, and rapid decomposition in the hot Mexican earth added to the identification problem. The sickly-sweet odor of rotting flesh hung over the grim ossuaries, trailing outside after red-eyed relatives into the oppressive dry heat of the day.

While most of the Mexican victims were buried with little fanfare, by grieving families, across the Rio Grande in Texas more than one thousand people packed Our Lady of Lourdes Catholic Church, between Hitchcock and Santa Fe, to say a tearful farewell to Mark Kilroy, whose body was one of the first to be positively identified.

As they filed inside, mourners walked past two trees decorated with yellow ribbons by about 150 children from the church school in remembrance of the former altar boy. Father Juan Nicolau urged the mourners to join Mark's family in celebration instead of mourning. He said that while the family was praying and searching for their son and brother, Mark was in Heaven "celebrating Easter with Christ." Father Nicolau said that was why, "the mother asked me to celebrate the resurrection of Mark with Jesus Christ."

"Criminals killed (his) body, but they were not able to kill his spirit," the Priest declared. "He is alive."

Father Nicolau warned that Mark's killers had chosen the wrong god, and he conceded that he was worried about stories he had heard about Satanic activity among young people.

Mark's parents also addressed the mourners during the service expressing their appreciation for the help and compassion they had received. Pictures of Mark and several newspaper clippings were spread out on a church table draped in white, a final memorial to the 1986 high school graduate whose most ardent desire was to be a physician so that he could help others.

"We were proud of Mark, and we thank God for the way he was and the way we were with him," James Kilroy told the congregation. Speaking in a firm, clear voice, Kilroy told the audience that the family was no longer worried about Mark because he was with God.

The two bodies discovered on the collective farm two miles south of the Santa Elena Ranch were identified as Moises Castillo Vasquez and Hector

---

de la Fuente, whose blonde handsomeness earned him the nickname, "El Guero," — "The Blondie."

Because many of the victims excavated at the Santa Elena Ranch had been dead and buried for weeks or months, identification presented a gruesome challenge to forensic pathologists. Skulls had been smashed open and faces destroyed during the brutal slayings. In some instances family members were able to identify relatives only by a single piece of clothing. Fourteen-year-old Jose Luis Garza Luna was one of those. Although most of his head was missing, his parents recognized his football jersey. It was his favorite shirt.

Jose Luis's family was so poor they couldn't afford the 150,000 pesos (about $65) to have the youngster embalmed and placed in a body bag for burial. When reports of the family's plight reached Matamoros's sister city, the Brownsville Community Health Center provided $179 to buy a plain wooden coffin for the boy. Students, faculty and non-teaching staff members of the Rio Grande City High School collected another $300 after a teacher appealed over the intercom for donations to buy a body bag. Reporters for the *Brownsville Herald* delivered the money to the grateful family and Jose Luis's father said it would be used to put the boy's name on the tombstone and spruce up the grave.

The hard-working, devoutly Christian family was devastated by the tragedy. The boy's father said none of them would leave the house alone after discovery of Jose Luis's dreadful murder, and one daughter, a mute, refused to leave her room. A neighbor was talking about leaving his ranch and moving as far away from the horror as possible.

But like the Kilroys, Jose Luis's parents indicated they were satisfied that their son's suffering was over and his soul had moved on to a more pleasant existence where he could no longer be harmed. "He's in Heaven with God," the elder Garcia told a *Herald* reporter.

The art of identifying a body or determining the cause of death in a murder is called forensic science. Forensic researchers include coroners and specially trained police officers, and while it is far from an exact art, breakthroughs in medical technology are allowing practitioners to put a face on a skull or pinpoint the exact cause of death as never before.

Some artists specialize in a single intriguing aspect of forensic medicine, and it is they whom police agencies sometimes turn to when faced with a particularly puzzling case.

Forensic artists call on their artistic and deductive skills to sculpt clay faces on the shiny, bleached skulls of the unidentified dead. Armed with available information about sex, race, and age, the artists rebuild the flesh-like features over the bone and the victim becomes imminently more recognizable. Photos can be taken of the new faces and circulated among police agencies and the public with leaflets containing other suspected information about the victim and the crime.

The talents of a forensic artist in Oklahoma were so highly regarded that she was asked to sculpt the features of the long-dead Egyptian Pharaoh Tutankhamen, as well as nine of the thirty-three young men known to have been murdered by serial killer John Wayne Gacy near Chicago.

At the Florida State Museum, University of Florida, Gainesville, forensic anthropologists use a revolutionary video procedure to identify the remains of crime, suicide, and accident victims. The high-tech technique involves superimposing on a video screen X-rays of the victim's skull along with photographs taken during the lifetime of the person suspected of matching the remains. If the skull belongs to the person in the photos, the two images should fit like puzzle pieces.

Sauceda Galavan's body was identified by a related X-ray analysis of his left foot, which had been injured earlier. The twenty-two-year-old bachelor, chauffeur, and former Matamoros policeman's facial features had been destroyed by decomposition. But that was a rare case, because most of the victims were quickly identified by distraught family members.

As law enforcement agencies went about the job of identifying the remains dug up on the ranch, other lawmen began to investigate the possibility that a series of other terrible multiple killings along the border might be connected to Constanzo and his ruthless band of murderous drug smugglers.

In fact, the discovery of the thirteen bodies at the Santa Elena Ranch, and the others nearby, was the climax of two weeks of unprecedented drug-related slaughter along the U.S.-Mexico border. One U.S. Border Patrol sector chief called the Rio Grande Valley "the hottest smuggling spot, land or sea, in the nation." And heavy drug trafficking is accompanied by widespread violence!

In Cameron County, the murder rate tripled in a single year as drug smugglers converged to transport their product across the border. Anyone who tried to muscle their way into the territory of established gangs, and police who tried to slow the flow of drugs, had a fight on their hands.

The first of the mass slayings along the border came to light with the discovery on March 27, a few days after Mark Kilroy vanished from Matamoros, of five people found tortured and shot to death and stacked in a shed outside Tucson, Arizona. Two Americans were among the victims.

Only two days later, nine men and three women were discovered butchered on the abandoned Los Alamos Ranch in Agua Prieta, Mexico, a border city directly south of Douglas, Arizona. Like the others, the victims had been horribly tortured, strangled, hanged, stabbed and shot. Eight of the bodies were unceremoniously dumped down an abandoned, garbage-filled well, and four were buried and covered with lime in an earthen septic tank. A thirteenth body, that of a reputed drug dealer, was found about a month later only a few miles from the site of the Agua Prieta massacre. Like several of the victims at Agua Prieta, the face of the suspected drug dealer had been coated with lime to hasten decomposition.

Police officials in Agua Prieta, a thriving Mexican city of some 75,000 in the Mexican state of Sonara, said the murderers, many of whom used various aliases, apparently killed the twelve victims in an attempt to learn the identity of an informer. One of the women had her fingers cut off, and American police officials noted that was a classic gang punishment for informers. All the victims were thought to be gang members and were apparently slain after a series of botched smuggling attempts. In the brief period of a few weeks before the murders, U.S. drug enforcement agents broke up three separate drug running efforts and confiscated one hundred kilos of cocaine and more than $4 million in cash.

The bodies on the Santa Elena Ranch in Matamoros were discovered shortly after the initial find in Agua Prieta, leading police to speculate initially that there might be a link. Several factors connected the killings.

They all involved drug trafficking; victims at both locations had been mutilated and tortured; at least one victim at both locations was a police officer; in both cases, the murders followed smuggling operations gone awry; certain police officers in both Matamoros and Agua Prieta had been closely linked to drug trafficking; and some of the victims in both locations were suspected of being drug informants.

It looked good on paper, but the perceived association between the murder cases fell apart when Mexican police issued arrest warrants for eight people, including one American citizen, in the Agua Prieta torture-slayings. The reputed leader of the group, who used the nickname "The Tombstone," was eventually apprehended in a desert trailer home west of Tucson, and extradicted back to Mexico for trial. Telephone calls to the television show "America's Most Wanted," as well as a local crime hotline and confidential sources, were credited with helping to run down the suspect. Authorities identified "The Tombstone" as a cousin of the police chiefs in both Agua Prieta and Douglas.

The killings near Tucson, although also drug related, had no direct connection to the Matamoros case. U.S. Senator Dennis DeConcini, an Arizona Democrat, told reporters that he believed the infamous Medellin cocaine cartel headquartered in Columbia, South America, was tied to the slaughter in both Agua Prieta and Tucson. He suspected that the Tucson killings occurred when drugs were delivered but not paid for.

Sixteen days after the discovery of Mark Kilroy's body, police in Galveston, Texas, disclosed that two men being held in the Galveston County Jail on burglary charges had allegedly tried to bolster their sagging bank accounts by phoning the frantic family and telling them they had kidnapped Mark. The convicts reputedly promised to release him for a $10,000 ransom.

The demand, made exactly one week before Mark's body was recovered, bolstered the rapidly fading hopes of his family that he was still alive. Even Santa Fe Police Chief Mike Barry later admitted that at first he was heartened by the new development. But when a second call was received, he began to believe that he and the family were dealing with a cruel extortion attempt.

Investigators confirmed that suspicion and set a trap to capture the ghoulish crooks. Police said that a pay-phone in the jail was used in the effort to set up a meeting at which Helen Kilroy was to give $2,000 to outside accomplices of the prisoners. Another $8,000 was to be paid upon Mark's safe return.

The first meeting fell apart after the schemers spotted a police car in the area, but a second meeting was later arranged. The accused extortionists were said to have threatened to cut off Mark's fingers and mail them to the family if police arrested or followed the people the money was delivered to.

With police in on the plans, the Kilroys agreed to go along with the deal. Helen Kilroy drove to the prearranged site with $2,000 in cash beside her on the front seat of her car. Police monitoring the activity said they watched the suspects drive by the pickup spot before and after she arrived, but they never approached her car.

Police had traced the calls, however, and later arrested five people, including a woman and the two inmates, on extortion charges. One of the jail inmates was already in trouble for allegedly telephoning members of the family of Shelley Sikes and claiming he had a map that could lead them to the missing Texas City teenager's grave.

When news of the attempted shakedown was made public, Helen Kilroy expressed outrage that the two men already in jail were able to carry out the extortion attempt from behind bars. "We were absolutely shocked that people who are in prison for a good reason are able to call out and terrorize innocent people," she told reporters. "We were really shocked that people can be terrorized from inside our jails."

But neither Mrs. Kilroy nor the police should have been surprised at anything that transpired after Mark disappeared. The Kilroys had been watching their serene existence unravel since the day they learned that Mark was missing. Finding Mark was one thing. Finding the people responsible for his disappearance and murder was something else, and it wasn't an easy job, especially in Mexico.

The discovery of Mark Kilroy's body and the ensuing search for his killers dominated the front pages of newspapers in Mexico and South Texas for weeks, but the story eventually began to show up inside the papers, then to be left out altogether, despite efforts by law enforcement agencies determined to capture Constanzo and his gang. Other, more immediate local, national, and international news took its place. Some of the news was monotonously plebian.

In Brownsville, the police blotter showed a call to a house where a husband returned home from work and found his four children alone. Their mother was out drinking, so he locked her out of the house. Another call took police to a home where a burglar had stolen a television set and a portable radio. Hub caps were stolen from a 1988 Le Mans parked outside another home. And a woman reported that a boy selling tamales for two dollars ran off with her change after she handed him a twenty dollar bill.

On the drug scene, narcotics officers picked up five men, including two from Brownsville, while confiscating more than a ton of marijuana. About a third of the pot picked up in the drug sweep was secreted in a quarter ton military truck assigned to the U.S. Army Reserve.

As law enforcement agencies stepped up the international manhunt for Constanzo, on the border the healing process had begun. But Brownsville and its sister city, Matamoros, would never fully recover from the horror they had jointly experienced.

The menacing cloud of supernatural evil that hung over the Hell Ranch had yet to be dealt with and dispatched.

It was a sparkling sunlit Sunday afternoon and the ranch was nearly deserted. The horde of journalists had thinned and most had drifted back to their home cities to turn their attention to other matters. Only a handful of people were still hanging around, among them Sara's former TSC instructor, Zavaleta; Lieutenant Gavito; and Hildalgo Castillo, the father of one of the victims, when a five car caravan of *federales* pulled up to the ranch. As uniformed officers piled out cradling automatic weapons in their arms, a smallish brown-skinned man walked to the blood-splattered tarpaper shack. A boy who appeared to be about twelve or thirteen years old crouched a few feet away attending a cardboard box he had placed near him on the sun-parched ground, occasionally peering inside.

The little man sprinkled salt, powders and oils, mumbled incantations and made the sign of the cross inside the shack. Then as the *federales* nervously watched, he stepped outside and carefully circled the building, soberly repeating the meticulous ritual. Finished at last, he moved away from the building. *Federales,* waiting with five-gallon gasoline cans, splashed it with fuel and lit a match. As the shack burst into flames, several officers crossed themselves, and mumbled quick prayers invoking Christian protection. The shed seemed to groan in human agony. And the *federales* kept their eyes fixed on the burning building as if expecting to see the shadowy wraiths of demons or the agonized spirits of the young men who died there twisting and turning in the cleansing flames.

A photographer for the *Brownsville Herald* had driven up shortly before the shed was torched, and observed a man circling the shack. He was told that the man was performing an exorcism. The photographer quickly began snapping pictures.

Zavaleta, who also took video film of the bizarre purification ceremony, was later quoted by a reporter as saying of the policemen: "They looked like they were expecting an army of Satan to appear."

It took only a few minutes for the sun-dried shed to burn to the ground. When the last charred upright wall at last collapsed into the smoking black and gray rubble, the *curandero* turned and walked to the boy with the box. The old man and his apprentice peered inside at the white dove. If it was dead, its death would be reluctantly accepted as proof that the evil was too strong. But the bird was healthy and alive. The devil's fortress had been destroyed, and lingering new evils that might have been inflicted on the shaken community averted by the exorcism.

Mexican police were reluctant to discuss the exorcism. Asked about reports that valuable evidence — the oily cauldrons of human body parts and blood, goat heads, mutilated chickens, herbs, candles and other paraphernalia — had been destroyed, police responded that the concern was unfounded. They said the interior and exterior were photographed and all evidence removed before the shack was incinerated.

At the ranch, where the death shack had once stood, a wooden cross was laid on the ashes.

CHAPTER 12

The Manhunt

MEXICO IS A NATION overflowing with superstition and legend. Its citizens believe strongly in God and Satan, and if there was any doubt about the latter, the atrocities committed in Matamoros certainly set them straight.

One 400-year-old legend maintains that the devil is trapped for most of the year on Sierrita Santa Cruz, a towering mountain in La Junta de Los Rios, a stretch of river valley that extends from Presidio, Texas, to Ojinaga, Mexico.

According to the legend, the devil is held prisoner in his rocky mountaintop home by a cross erected by Spanish priests in the 16th Century. It is speculated that the padres erected the cross as a way of capturing the hearts, minds and souls of the Indians living in the area. The Indians firmly believed that evil spirits inhabited the mountains, and were the cause of any misfortune that befell them. The priests cunningly manipulated the fear of the spirits to convert the hapless Indians to Catholicism, promising that the powerful Christian religious symbol would keep the mischievous spirits at bay forever.

However, once a year — usually five days before Holy Cross Day, the first Sunday in May — the cross is brought down from the mountaintop in a solemn ceremony so that their homes and crops can be protected by allowing Satan to walk the land for five days and observe the faithful praying to God. At the end of five days, the cross is returned to its original spot, trapping Satan for another year in his foreboding mountain home.

In 1989, Satan wasn't living on Sierrita Santa Cruz. After a brief yet murderous stint in Matamoros, he fled into the night with the police hot on his trail. The Prince of Darkness had taken the name Adolfo de Jesus Constanzo.

On April 11, the handsome, charismatic cult leader learned that police had closed in on the gang's isolated ranch hideout in Matamoros. He knew what they would find and that he would be exposed as the leader of the killer cult.

But Constanzo had already made plans for his escape. The accused gang members picked up at the Hell Ranch were already spewing out the gang's secrets to police, but Constanzo was determined to escape capture. He was convinced that he was too smart to fall into the hands of police.

Before fleeing the Brownsville Holiday Inn with Sara and a handful of his other most trusted followers, Constanzo telephoned his mother in Miami and told her he had to run. He assured her that he was innocent of whatever terrible crimes might be blamed on him. But he said he had to flee because he was afraid that cruel Mexican police would torture him, she later told reporters. Sara telephoned the physical education office at TSC and said she wouldn't be coming in anymore. She had some personal problems to work out.

Constanzo's mother said she tried to talk her son into facing the consequences, but he wouldn't listen.

"I have to run, Mom," he reputedly told her. "I am innocent, but I have to hide. Do not believe what you see on television, all the terrible things. I can't tell you any more. I'm sorry."

Constanzo's mother and his thirteen-year-old sister had visited him in Mexico during the Christmas holidays. Everything seemed perfectly normal. She and the girl stayed at Adolfo's home and met his friends. They were pleasant and gentlemanly. There was no hint of the dark actions that would later be blamed on them by law enforcement agencies in two countries.

It may have been the deceptive facade of normalcy that made it so difficult for her to accept accusations that her doting son and his polite companions had butchered fifteen men and boys in an unholy bloodbath.

A full-blown international manhunt was launched for the charismatic cult leader. He had disappeared even as the bodies were being unearthed at the Santa Elena Ranch. But investigators were determined that he would not get away with his crimes.

In a massive joint operation employing hundreds of officers, the Mexican Federal Judicial Police joined with a task force of United States authorities that included local police and sheriff's officers, the Border Patrol, DEA, Customs Service, and the FBI.

Law enforcement agencies on both sides of the border, however, had few immediate solid leads to the whereabouts of Constanzo and his companions. The Godfather and Sara were seen driving around Brownsville in a new $80,000 luxury car on April 11, the day after the discovery of the first bodies at the Hell Ranch, then they vanished.

The FBI filed charges of Interstate Flight to avoid prosecution against the Godfather and Sara.

The Cameron County Sheriff's Department had issued an all-points bulletin for the apprehension of the *Padrino* and his suspected female companion. And police in Matamoros and Brownsville were picking up plenty of tips. They all had to be checked out.

Police in Miami and other South Florida communities posted flyers with Constanzo's photograph and description, as well as pictures of Sara, in squad rooms and detective bureaus, when reports circulated that he was on his way there to see his family.

Other reports indicated that Constanzo had burrowed deep into the criminal underground of Mexico City, hidden by friends. There were other whispers that the fugitives were hiding out in Guadalajara. And there were even stories that they were driving to Illinois after authorities in Brownsville learned they had friends in Chicago. As a result, Illinois State Police were given a description of a Ford Taurus Constanzo was believed to be driving north. Authorities were told that the $10,000 1988 model car was Sara's, and that she had paid cash for it.

There was speculation as well that the suspected cultists had driven to Houston, where they were believed to have strong ties with other gang members and drug traffickers.

The FBI and Houston Police suspected that the cultists might be connected to 436 pounds of cocaine, worth about $20 million, confiscated from a "safe house" on the northwest side of the city by local and federal authorities the previous June. An altar strewn with candles, knives, chalices, the statue of a male figure, and other ritual paraphernalia similar to the equipment found at the ranch had been found at the site of the police raid. Investigators had also learned that Constanzo had made several large purchases the previous year in Houston, including luxury automobiles. An FBI spokesman indicated that the agency had been aware of the gang's activities in the Houston area for some time. Police also began investigating possible gang connections to hundreds of pounds of cocaine seized in two other raids in the Houston suburb of Pasadena, and in Corpus Christi the previous July.

None of the tips led police to Constanzo, his reputed witch or to his other suspected accomplices.

In Mexico City, police spent days tracing Constanzo's rise through Mexico's upper class, fascinated by his uncanny ability to meet and woo the right people.

The free spending *brujo*'s suspected criminal activities had enabled him to accumulate huge amounts of cash, and investigators suspected that he may have hidden a small fortune in Mexico and the United States. Although Constanzo's mother said her son sent her only small amounts of money, police claimed information indicating that he had a bank account in Miami with substantial deposits. Wherever he was hiding out, police believed, it was unlikely he would be short of cash.

As investigators patiently worked to piece together a picture of Constanzo's life and acquaintances, they received hundreds of sightings of the fugitives. Each of the reports, no matter how flimsy, was carefully checked out.

Investigators realized that Constanzo could run, and he could hide — but he and his companions couldn't elude the manhunt forever.

Mexican police learned that Constanzo had several residences, including a fashionable home in an upper class suburban neighborhood of Mexico City, and two nearby apartments. All three of the homes were thoroughly searched by officers in a desperate effort to find clues.

Constanzo was used to the very best, and his home in Atizapan de Zaragoza, a pleasant, quiet upper class suburb eleven or twelve miles northeast of Mexico City, was an example of his appreciation for opulence.

It was also a testament to his paranoia and fear of discovery. The attractive white stucco house was protected by a ten-foot high wall, heavy metal gates, a remote control surveillance system with five monitor screens, and motion activated spotlights that illuminated the yard whenever a car drove by at night.

Police, armed with submachine guns, raided the home and found the walls splattered with blood and littered with the remains of animals, apparently used in religious services. Two altars similar to those found on the Matamoros ranch were discovered in the house, along with a huge wardrobe of designer clothing, fine furniture, a large, color television set, and other expensive electronic equipment. A pockmarked handgun target was confiscated from the garage.

Another ritual altar, made of marble, was also discovered in Constanzo's apartment on Jalapa Street, in the quiet, middle class Roma district of downtown Mexico City. Police also found a book filled with male names and photographs of Constanzo. The photographs and book were confiscated, and officers began checking out the names in efforts to identify additional cultists or drug traffickers. The names of Martin Quintana and Omar Ochoa were among those listed within the book.

Constanzo's neighbors in the fashionable Mexico City suburb of Atizapan were stunned when armed police raided his home there. It was directly across from an elementary school.

Constanzo and a few male friends had moved into the home several months before, claiming to be college students. No women had ever been seen at the house, although some neighbors suspected the pleasant young men were animal lovers because they kept a dog. The "students" had left mysteriously in the middle of the night on April 10 or 11, loading boxes into a car, then driving quietly away into the darkness.

Constanzo, who favored expensive luxury cars, had been a model neighbor, keeping his home clean and his yard spruced up with a flowering garden. He seldom talked with his neighbors, but when he did, he was always very polite.

Shortly after police raided his house and apartments, then sealed them off with armed guards, other uniformed officers raided and sealed off the homes of suspected cult members Omar Francesco Orea Ochoa and Martin Quintana Rodriguez. Orea and Quintana were on the run with the *El Padrino* and *La Padrina*. Both men had long departed their homes, however, and the raids produced no clues to a possible destination.

While the search for the cultists progressed, the Hell Ranch had become a tourist attraction. Curiosity-seekers walked around the sun-scorched grounds, awed by the nearness of such terrible death, and stared in embarrassed fascination at the stinking, maggot-infested cauldrons that still sat in the doorway of the shack where the murders were celebrated.

"Curiosity brought me here, nothing more," one tourist awkwardly confirmed to a newsman. "I don't have any interests like this," he apologized. "These are unbelievable things."

When asked about the growing stream of curious onlookers, police in Matamoros simply shook their heads. There was nothing they could do; nothing that needed to be done. For many, a visit to the Santa Elena Ranch was a cathartic experience helpful in dispelling the fear that had possessed them since the murders became public.

As police on both sides of the Rio Grande stepped up their manhunt, U.S. Customs agents confirmed that the search marked one of the most intensive efforts in the history of the border area.

In Starr County, Texas, federal and local officers raided three ranches after word spread that Sara and Constanzo had been seen in the vicinity.

The rumor was spurred by a Starr County official who believed he had seen Sara at a convenience store in nearby La Gloria, a small, predominantly Mexican-American community in the northern part of the county. He told police that after he had driven in, his attention was drawn by a "tall, strikingly beautiful" fair-skinned young woman driving a gray automobile. She was talking on a pay-phone in front of the store, and her light skin and sophisticated air caused him to study her closely.

After the suspicious bureaucrat left the store, the young woman's image continued to haunt him. He thought she looked familiar, but was unable to immediately match a name with the face. That night when a picture of Sara was shown on a television newscast, he realized that the reputed cult priestess bore a striking resemblance to the woman he had seen using the pay telephone. And although he couldn't identify the make of the gray car the woman was driving, police believed Constanzo had fled in a gray 1989 Mercedes Benz sedan.

Adding fuel to suspicions that the fugitives might be in the area were rumors of cult-like activities — including animal sacrifices — at a barren ranch surrounded by mesquite and prickly pear near Delmita, about four miles from San Isidro.

Based on that information, FBI agents from the McAllen and Browns-ville offices, supported by members of the Starr County Sheriff's Department and the Border Patrol, moved quickly on the Delmita Ranch and two others in the area. Officers were armed with machine guns and shotguns, and backed up by a low flying observation plane overhead, but no suspects were found in any of the raids. FBI agents were philosophical about the frustrating turn of events, noting that they had to check out every lead, no matter how skimpy.

While the police were scouring the Rio Grande Valley and Mexico for Constanzo and his companions, an ecumenical, community-wide prayer service was held in Brownsville in an attempt to "heal the land" and encourage local citizens to put the tragic events behind them and get on with their lives. Several churches from throughout Brownsville participated in the ceremony, as did Brownsville Mayor Ygnacio Garza and Police Chief Andres Vega, Jr.

On April 18, a U.S. grand jury in McAllen, Texas, indicted Constanzo, Sara and nine other suspects on drug charges that ranged from conspiracy to import marijuana to possession with intent to distribute. The charges would allow U.S. officials to arrest the fugitives in the United States and extradite them to Mexico, where they could be tried for murder.

A few days later, a Mexican federal judge in Matamoros told reporters he felt there was "abundant proof" that the four cult members arrested earlier at the Santa Elena Ranch and suspected in the bloody killings there were guilty of the crimes charged against them.

So convinced was Judge Francisco Salvador Perez that Elio Hernandez Rivera, Sergio Martinez, David Serna Valdez and Serafin Hernandez Garcia were guilty of participating in the ritual slayings at the cult's ranch hideout, that he refused to allow them to post bond. In addition to the killings, the four men were accused of arms law violations, illegal burying of dead bodies, drug trafficking and kidnapping.

Some of the suspects denied participating in the slayings, but Perez said he believed they were still responsible because they were members of a drug smuggling organization that killed innocent people.

Police grilled the four accused cult members already in custody for information about the whereabouts of their leader, but despite the massive manhunt Constanzo and Sara somehow managed to stay one jump ahead of the law.

Law enforcement authorities knew quite a bit about Constanzo, his connections and early life, but Sara Aldrete turned out to be a true mystery woman. Police, family and friends discovered, much to their horror, that the attractive coed was a quiet, industrious college student by day, and was apparently the priestess of a murderous cult of drug smugglers by night. No

Hollywood script writer could have added a more bizarre twist to an already macabre situation.

As Police combed the nation for Sara, her parents, Israel and Teresa Aldrete, loyally insisted that their daughter was innocent, and expressed shock at her alleged cult activities. The news was too horrifying for the family to accept, and Israel Aldrete, an electrician, said he found it mentally impossible to work. The heartbroken couple were helped by the kindness of neighbors, all of whom knew Sara as a kind, thoughtful girl — not the heartless co-leader of one of the Mexican-American border's most blood thirsty gangs.

Sara's parents were investigated and interviewed repeatedly by the police, but they maintained that they were completely unaware of her cult involvement until officers searched her bedroom and found a ritual altar, blood-splattered walls and several votive candles.

Israel Aldrete said Sara never showed any interest in occult activities. She was a good student and loving daughter who usually came home immediately after class, and didn't go out very much.

But she wasn't unpopular. Sara had many friends, both male and female, who behaved like friendly, normal young people. "There was nothing strange in the way she lived," Sara's father said.

Students and faculty members who knew Sara at TSC, which was within walking distance of the International Bridge in Brownsville, were equally baffled at Sara's apparent involvement in the murderous drug gang.

They knew Sara as an honors student. Anthony Zavaleta, a sociology and anthropology instructor who has studied the occult for many years, had Sara as a student in some of his classes, and said he never noticed her exhibit any of the overt signs likely to be seen in people involved in cult or ritualistic activities.

Other teachers shared a similar view of Sara, noting that she was a hard working student who often offered to help classmates whenever they needed it.

An English teacher said the suspected cult member always saw the best in everyone and was always eager to please, sometimes too much so. The teacher suggested that Sara's eagerness to please may have hinted at a problem, and could indicate that Sara was naive and easily duped.

But a few students who knew Sara said she had mentioned interest in the occult.

As police investigated Sara's life, they uncovered one bizarre development after another.

For example, one of the law officers leading the manhunt for the fugitive cultists, Cameron County Sheriff Alex Perez, had been the justice of the peace who had officiated at her wedding in 1983, when she was nineteen.

Police knew that Sara had fled the same time as Constanzo, and it was immediately assumed that the duo were traveling together. But when a purse, passport, $15,000 and other items belonging to Sara were found in a safe house in Mexico City, investigators suspected that Constanzo may have killed his priestess. They speculated she may have known too much about the drug smuggling operation and cult killings, and was murdered to keep her quiet. If Constanzo had, indeed, killed his long-legged companion she might be buried or otherwise disposed of somewhere in Mexico City, some officers believed.

The four cult suspects in custody in Matamoros were shaken by the rumors and news reports of Sara's execution. They knew too much, and had already talked too much. And they were terrified of reprisals by *El Padrino* and other cultists still on the loose, either in the form of supernatural attacks or physical assassination. They demanded more protection and the already tight security around them was strengthened. They were also isolated from other prisons.

Few American lawmen bought the idea, however. They were convinced that Sara was still very much alive, and that the discovery of the purse and other personal items was deliberately set up by the fugitives to throw police off her trail — and the trail of Constanzo.

The manhunters believed that if Sara and Constanzo were still travelling or hiding out together, she would be the most visible and easily spotted because of her unusual height. Constanzo, on the other hand, had no such easily distinguishable features and his physical appearance was probably not too dissimilar to that of the majority of young men in Mexico or the U.S.

Police vowed to continue the all-out search for Sara, until definitive proof of her death was turned up. Nothing less would be acceptable.

Meanwhile, police in Mexico City had uncovered disturbing signs that some of the Matamoros killer gang members might be linked to at least eight unsolved killings in the capital city in 1987. The victims — five men and three women — were found on the bottom of a river just outside the nation's capital. The bodies were discovered following a tip that a housekeeper had disappeared after telling friends she was going to a black mass.

Like the bodies discovered in Matamoros, all eight victims had been cut open, organs removed and their bodies horribly and viciously mutilated. They were then bound to cement blocks with lengths of heavy wire and dispatched in the river.

Police strongly suspected that the eight victims were murdered by the gang because of the ritualistic manner of their murder and dismemberment.

As the investigation of Constanzo's Mexico City connection burgeoned, police speculated that small splinter sects might be spreading out from the mother cult led by the *Padrino*. Officers feared that as new members were recruited into the unholy alliance, senior members were apparently ordained "godfathers" or "godmothers" and instructed to teach the recruits about the cult and its demonic association.

By this time, the cultists were being sought in connection with more than twenty murders in the Matamoros and Mexico City areas, and police were uncertain where the grisly investigation would eventually lead — or when it would end.

As the manhunt continued into the first part of May, an increasing number of tips placed Constanzo and Sara in Mexico City, and that is where the Federal Judicial Police and local lawmen began to concentrate most of their search efforts.

As police narrowed their manhunt for the leaders of the cult responsible for some of the most heinous and widely publicized murders in Mexican history, the rest of the nation was gearing up for the annual *Cinco de Mayo* (May 5) celebration.

Many people believe *Cinco de Mayo* is Mexican Independence Day, but in fact the festival commemorates a battle in 1862 in which 4,850 poorly armed and undertrained teenage Mexican soldiers soundly defeated a supposedly superior French invasion force of more than 8,000 soldiers just east of Mexico City.

The Mexican defenders suffered only 250 casualties while one-eighth of the French force was killed or wounded. The battle, a small footnote in world history at best, ended European dreams of a French empire on Mexican soil. Now 100 years later, the celebration of that victory provided a reason to party for ninety million Mexicans, and more than twelve million Mexican-Americans.

The 1989 *Cinco de Mayo* celebration in Mexico City was shaping up to be something spectacular, but police were finding it difficult to concentrate on the upcoming holiday. They had developed some important clues that seemed to pinpoint the whereabouts of Constanzo.

This time the reputed drug godfather and killer cultist would not escape.

Press conference after discovery

The ongoing search for evidence.

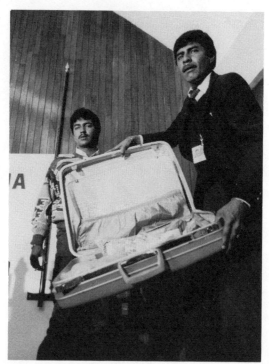

Cache of drugs

One of many hideouts

Locals involved in disappearances

The fourth floor apartment where shootout occurred.

CHAPTER 13

A Shootout in Mexico City

THE RESIDENTS OF MEXICO CITY were still basking in the pleasure of the recent *Cinco de Mayo* celebration a day earlier, when a team of police officers spread out through the Cuautemoc neighborhood to check out reports that an unusually tall, light-skinned woman resembling the fugitive Sara Aldrete had been seen grocery shopping in the area.

And there had been other stories, of several young men who had quietly moved into an apartment in the neighborhood only three or four blocks from the U.S. Embassy and begun to attract the attention of neighbors with their strange habits. For one thing, they bought large amounts of groceries, but preferred to make several trips back-and-forth from the stores carrying the food themselves, rather than use the services of a bag boy. And it apparently wasn't money that was keeping them from asking for help, because they had been flashing large bankrolls of U.S. money. American dollars were rarely seen outside the Zona Rosa and other tourist areas, and especially not in such large amounts.

Cuautemoc is near the center of Mexico City and is a comfortable step up from middle class, but it is also a neighborhood like those in most cities where local residents and business people know each other by name or sight and strangers can be as obvious objects of curiosity as they would be in any small town. And the tall woman and young men had attracted attention.

It was about two in the afternoon when a pair of Mexican Federal Judicial Police officers stopped to investigate a car parked at the curb near the intersection of Rio Sena and the Paseo de la Reforma, the city's busiest thoroughfare. Passersby offered the information that the luxury car had been there for several days, and it seemed possible that it might have been abandoned.

Although it was the hottest part of the day, the street was typically busy. The neighborhood boasted an attractive array of restaurants and stores and shoppers were still diligently going about their business. A customer had just stopped to buy a tamale and a soft drink from a street peddler when the officers stepped off the curb to peer inside the car.

The activities of the lawmen hadn't gone unnoticed. Inside the fourth-floor apartment just opposite the parked car, Adolfo de Jesus Constanzo was nervously watching them. Despite his loyal ring of followers, his ruthless and crafty mind, his riches, and his powerful black magic spells, the police were outside. And they were looking for him. Constanzo lost his nerve. He went berserk.

Alvaro de Leon Valdez was asleep when he was awakened by Constanzo's screaming. "They're here! Why run? Don't hide!!" the Godfather screeched. He was hysterical.

"All is lost! All is lost!," he screamed. "This money is not going to be for anyone!"

He ordered his frightened companions to scoop up the currency stashed around the apartment in piles of pesos, U.S. $20, $50 and $100 bills, and gold coins. As they handed it to him, he ripped open the window, and tossed the money into the street, yelling, "Take this, you poor fools!"

Moments later, while startled passersby began to scramble for the unexpected shower of riches flowing from the upper floor of the apartment building, Constanzo shoved the ugly barrel of a machine gun out the window and began spewing a wild spray of bullets at the two policemen. The officers dove for cover behind the car, and the tamale vendor and his customers sprinted for safety. A vegetable vendor crouching behind yet another parked car watched in horror as his cart was chopped into jagged chunks of kindling, and the produce was reduced to useless garbage by the spray of bullets.

One man scrambling after the shower of currency was nicked by one of the bullets, and slumped to the sidewalk. Moments later he was pulled to safety by another passerby.

The police officers were untouched, although the shower of bullets exploded all around them, shattering the car windows, tearing through the metal sides, and ripping huge chunks of concrete from the street and sidewalk. Their escape from the furious attack by the screaming fugitive seemed almost miraculous.

The officers had been caught completely by surprise, and had Constanzo not panicked, they may have merely peered idly into the car and moved on. Later accounts of their activities before Constanzo began firing on them varied, however.

Police said they descended on the neighborhood as part of a stepped up manhunt through specific sections of Mexico City, but some of Constanzo's neighbors maintained that officers didn't show up until after receiving telephone calls about angry shouts and gunshots coming from the fourth floor.

One neighbor who lived next door to Constanzo later recounted that she had heard a loud argument within the cult leader's room and what sounded like a woman's voice yelling, "Kill him," followed by six gunshots. All of this, the neighbor insisted, occurred before police arrived.

A street corner juice vendor described hearing a loud argument with vulgar name calling. "I'm sure someone called police," he said.

Whether or not police were notified of Constanzo's whereabouts or merely stumbled on his last hideout in a stroke of unbelievable luck may never be known. But what followed the Godfather's sudden attack was an intense 45-minute battle.

Temporarily outgunned, the police officers crouching behind the car returned the fusillade of fire erupting from the apartment with their handguns, while shouting for civilians to clear the streets. Incredibly, even in the reasonably affluent neighborhood, several people continued to dash through the gunfire, risking their lives to gather up the windswept currency from the street and sidewalks.

Police switchboards were lighting up with calls, and minutes after the first staccatto belch of gunfire, reinforcements were streaming into the neighborhood. Patrol cars with heavily armed uniform officers were dashing down the Paseo de la Reforma and screeching to a stop a couple blocks from the apartment. Guns drawn, the officers scrambled from the cars and, combat style, worked their way closer to the firefight.

Street intersections blocks from the corner of the Rio Sena and the Paseo de la Reforma were blocked off with other cars and hastily erected wooden barricades. Other lawmen worked to clear civilians from the sidewalks in the immediate neighborhood. Most of the civilians stepped into stores, or apartment house foyers, where they found windows that permitted them to continue watching the shootout.

A specially trained corp of officers outfitted with bullet-proof vests, automatic weapons and rifles with sniper scopes took up position facing the apartment and added their firepower to that of the police already there.

Some of Constanzo's male companions had joined him at the windows. Crouching behind walls, they would suddenly shove the barrels of their weapons out the window, empty a clip of cartridges in a wild burst of fire, then scuttle back out of sight to catch their breath and reload. Sara was screaming to stop shooting or the police would kill them all.

Nearly every structure in the dusty, sunlit block was hit as the hail of gunfire criss-crossed the street.

After forty-five minutes of wild firing the cultists began to run out of ammunition and police, who had sustained only one minor injury during the battle, took advantage of the lull in the action. They were preparing to storm the apartment, which had grown suddenly quiet, when Sara Aldrete, her long hair matted with sweat and dirt, ran screaming outside. "He's dead!" she shrieked, "They killed him! He's dead!"

Burly policemen clattered up the stairs where three more cultists cowered, faces flushed and frightened, with their hands in the air. Omar Francesco Orea Ochoa's saucer eyes brimmed with tears. His body trembled uncontrollably. A middle-aged woman, later identified as forty-three-year-old Maria del Rocio Cuevas Guerra was also shaking with sobs and fear. The ex-fashion model had already been known as an associate of Constanzo's, and was often referred to by gang members as "Carla."

The other survivor was Alvaro de Leon Valdez. The sullen, broad-shouldered young man had a reputation in the Matamoros border area as a fearless *pistolero*. Police had captured "El Duby."

The Godfather — and his current lover-bodyguard, Martin Quintana Rodriquez — were dead. Their bullet-riddled bodies were slumped together in a blood-splashed bedroom closet. Blood and pieces of flesh dripped from the walls. Both men were wearing shorts.

Several handguns, as well as Israeli Uzis and other automatic weapons were scattered around the shattered apartment. Hundreds of empty shell casings littered the floor, furniture was overturned and the walls were chewed up with bullet holes. Despite the terrible destruction, however, the apartment still showed signs of Constanzo's lifelong fastidiousness. In the kitchen, pots and pans were in place, cereal boxes and cans of food were neatly lined upon shelves and in cabinets. Items in the bathroom and other living spaces had been arranged with similar care.

Police also found burned and scorched currency, and a vast collection of bizarre items in the modest apartment, including red and white votive candles, black robes, two swords, a plastic skull, a rattlesnake rattle, dolls and other paraphernalia used in black magic ceremonies. All of it confirmed the worst suspicions of superstitious police — the drug runners were in league with the devil.

One of the suspects, twenty-nine-year-old Maria de Lourdes Bueno Lopez, was arrested the day after the shootout. But two other reputed gang members believed to have escaped during the shootout, as well as several other suspected cultists, were still being sought.

During the first few hours after the shootout that rocked the quiet residential neighborhood, police officers informed the press that Constanzo and Rodriquez had been killed in the exchange of gunfire. It wasn't until the dust began to settle and the facts became clearer, that it was discovered Constanzo had actually died at the hands of one of his own men — and at his own insistence. The bullet-riddled bodies of Constanzo and Quintana Rodriquez were taken to the central city morgue for autopsies. The survivors were moved under heavy guard to the Miguel Hidalgo district police station in the capitol's west side. There, questioning disclosed that Constanzo had ordered his own execution. He didn't want to be captured, and wanted to die with his lover.

The exhausted suspects were paraded before reporters during a press conference at the Mexico City attorney general's office the day after the shootout. They were placed behind a 3-by-6-foot table loaded with rattles, dolls, weapons, candles and other confiscated cult items, including black ritual clothing. The candles had been lighted.

Journalists had hurried to Mexico City from throughout Mexico and the United States, and others were still arriving at the airport. The shootout and the breakup of the *Narcosatanicos* gang was the most dramatic news to occur in the world's largest metropolis since the devastating killer earthquake of 1985.

The prisoners paraded in with their heads down. When Mexican reporters shouted at them to look at the cameras, they dutifully moved together in a line and posed with heads up. As a stern police official called their names, each of the prisoners held up a hand. Even though her shoulders slumped, the pale and haggard Sara towered over her companions. One of "El Duby's" eyes was red and swollen. Responding to reporters' questions, he said he had fallen at police headquarters.

It was at the press conference that de Leon Valdez and Sara discussed the final moments of Adolfo.

After throwing stacks of money out the window and shooting at the startled police officers, the survivors recounted, Constanzo let his companions continue the battle. As his followers kept up the fire from the windows, he stumbled around the apartment in a daze. The stunning realization that his ruthless reign of terror was over was slowly sinking in.

Knowing that escape was impossible, Constanzo decided that death was preferable to imprisonment and begged de Leon Valdez to kill him and Martin Quintana Rodriquez. Exhausted, Quintana agreed to the plan for suicide by execution.

"He ordered (de Leon Valdez) to kill him because it was the end and he wanted to die with Martin," Sara quietly explained during the press conference.

De Leon Valdez was reluctant to kill his beloved leader, but Constanzo, his anger and rage boiling over, was insistent. It was his time to die, he said, and he didn't want it to happen at the hands of police. And "El Duby," after all, had been ordained an executioner priest.

"He told me to kill him. I didn't want to, but he said I was going to have a tough time in hell if I didn't. He pleaded with me," explained de Leon Valdez, as he described the frenzied final minutes in the shattered apartment. "He slapped me twice in the face. We could hear the cops outside shooting. A lot of shots could be heard."

Bearded with dirty shoulder-length blonde hair, and wearing a soiled white shirt, de Leon Valdez told reporters that Constanzo gave him an Uzi, then sat down on a stool in the spacious bedroom closet. Martin kneeled at his side, and the Godfather ordered "El Duby" to do what had to be done.

It was over in a heartbeat. "I just stood there in front of them and pressed the trigger," de Leon Valdez confessed. "That was it."

After spraying Constanzo and Rodriquez with bullets, de Leon Valdez lurched dazedly to the window and continued firing at the police below until he ran out of ammunition.

While de Leon Valdez offered some dramatic surprises with his detailed account of Constanzo's final moments, most of the attention at the press conference was on Sara, the group's reputed "godmother."

Dressed in a purple and black T-shirt and a brown leather bomber's jacket, Sara stoically faced the cameras and microphones. She appeared more frightened than confident, and she trembled slightly as she told reporters that she had not been directly involved in the fifteen gruesome killings in Matamoros.

Bombarded by reporters' questions, Sara wavered between apologizing to the victims' families and saying she didn't know what she had gotten herself into when she first hooked up with Constanzo in 1987. She responded to questions from North Americans in nearly flawless English. Mexican and Central and South American journalists were addressed in Spanish.

"I don't know how I got involved," the statuesque Latin beauty stammered. "It was like knowing everything was one thing, then having it be something else."

Police, aware of Sara's relationship and brief romance with the bisexual gang leader, said they doubted her statement of innocence regarding the sacrificial killings. Other members of the cult told investigators that Sara was an equal partner with Constanzo, although de Leon Valdez said, during the press conference, that Sara never actually participated in the murders. The killing, he said, was usually done by Constanzo himself.

Asked by reporters what she would say to Mark Kilroy's family were she to meet them, Sara replied, "I feel sorry for them because when he disappeared I was trying to help him . . . If I would have known that it was like this, I would not have (joined the cult)." She refused to elaborate on what she meant when she said she was trying to "help" the missing American college student at the time of his disappearance. But some journalists speculated she may have been referring to her reputed activities helping to circulate leaflets and posters noting his disappearance and asking for information about his whereabouts.

Sara also used the press conference to vent her outrage at television reports following discovery of the bodies at the Santa Elena Ranch, accusing her of playing an integral role in the growth and control of the cult.

"When all the sacrifices were made, when all those things came out on television, all of those weren't true," she said firmly.

As she was being led away after the Sunday press conference, Sara told the crowd of reporters, photographers, and police that she had been afraid of Constanzo. A reporter then asked if she had loved the vicious cult leader. Shaking her head vigorously, Sara stared at the ground and said, "No, I didn't love him. But I followed him."

Unsurprising for a group of criminals eager to save themselves, the stories told to police and the press by the accused cult members began to change and mutate almost immediately.

During a second press conference in a small auditorium in the Mexico City attorney general's office on Monday, Sara told reporters that Constanzo literally held her prisoner after the murders were discovered on the Santa Elena Ranch.

"It was like hell," Sara said. "They treated me like a prisoner. I was scared. I don't know how I got into this without knowing what it was."

Asked by a reporter if she had witnessed the sacrificial murder of American college student Mark Kilroy, Sara, wearing the same black T-shirt and brown jacket from the day before, grimaced in disgust and shook her head.

"No, *señor*, she replied softly. "In my life, and I swear at this moment, that I never participated in any of the sacrifices, including that of American Mark Kilroy. Never! Never! If I had known what it was all about, I would never have gotten involved with them. No way."

"The first I learned of it was on TV. And (Constanzo) turned to me and said, 'They found them.' I said, 'What do you mean?' Eventually he told me everything, how he did it and why he did it."

"They brought me here because they knew that I knew where his house was located. He kept me there — he wouldn't let me go. It was like hell. It was so horrible. They held me here, treating me like a prisoner." Sara said at least nine cult members moved from place to place for about three weeks before settling in the apartment in Mexico City where police later found them.

Sara later claimed that even though she was not under continual surveillance by the Godfather and sometimes left the gang hideout for shopping or private moments, she feared going to police because he had threatened to harm her family with witchcraft. She said that Constanzo beat and kicked her when she talked about turning herself in, and held her by force and fear. One time when the gang was moving from one location to another in the Mexico City area and she pleaded to leave, Constanzo told her, "You don't leave here any way but dead, since you are a loose cannon."

Nevertheless, barely two hours before the shootout, she said she managed to drop a note outside the apartment to a boy on the street. The note, which was later turned over to prosecutors, said a woman was being held hostage and pleaded for help.

"El Duby" corroborated Sara's insistence that she had not participated in the slaughter. He told reporters: "What she said was true. These reports (of Sara's participation in the murders) are lies. She was never involved in it. I was present at some of the sacrifices, including (Mark) Kilroy, but she was not." "El Duby" said he and others sometimes sat quietly at a table watching *El Padrino* mutilate the bodies of victims.

However, days later Sara changed her story again and admitted involvement in some of the ritual slayings at the ranch in Matamoros. But investigators with the Mexico City attorney general's office were unsure how to take Sara's confession because the accused "godmother" of the cult had begun to show disturbing signs of a split personality. As the days wore on, three separate personas became evident — one for police, one for the television cameras and a third that emerged when she talked to herself.

U.S. Customs Service agent Oran Neck told a reporter with the *Houston Chronicle* just days after Sara's arrest that she had lost touch with reality. He said that she was demonstrating a dual personality. When she talks without TV cameras around, she is pretty truthful, he observed. Neck said that she was providing a lot of information and detail to investigators, but when cameras were around, she sort of reverted "back to this nice, young, clean-cut kid from Texas Southmost College."

Cameron County Sheriff's investigator Lt. George Gavito dourly observed that when cameras were around she was real nice. But when she was alone with police, she was "the same ol' witch." Gavito maintained a policeman's skepticism about the suspects, including Sara, and during the manhunt he had warned that both she and Constanzo were very dangerous. "They could kill for any reason," he cautioned.

Over the next several days Mexican and American authorities concentrated on netting cult members who had eluded the initial manhunt. And American authorities, who had filed drug trafficking indictments against the suspected gang members, in case they tried to slip north across the border, expressed relief that the criminals were nearly all apprehended in Mexico.

The group had committed the murders in Mexico, Oran Neck explained, which meant that if they had been apprehended in the United States, they could not be charged for those bloody crimes.

"The only reason we were looking for them was so we could extradite them to Mexico so they could be tried there," added FBI agent Bob Nixon, who was in on the international manhunt. "The purpose of the drug indictments here was to have probable cause to pick them up."

Nearly two weeks after the first press conference, Sara dropped a bombshell in an interview copyrighted by the *Houston Post* at the Eastern

Prison in Mexico City when she claimed she had been tortured by Mexican police and forced to sign a confession she had not read.

Two days after she was taken to police headquarters, a group of eight police officers blindfolded her and took her to another location, where she was tortured for most of the night, Sara said.

She alleged that during the torture she was administered painful electric shocks, beaten, nearly suffocated and "almost" raped. She charged that the torture was instigated because police were dissatisfied with the information she had given them, calling it "pure filler" and nothing worthwhile. The prisoner said that when the abuse became unbearable, she placated the police officers by enhancing her stories with made-up details even though she maintained she was innocent.

In another behind bars on-camera interview with Rafael Abramoritz of the Fox television network's show, "The Reporters," Sara repeated her charges of torture. She claimed police were attempting to force her to admit acts she didn't commit. And she said they wanted her to discuss matters she knew nothing about.

Appearing wane and washed out, with her long hair hanging limply onto her shoulders, Sara clasped the bars of her cell while accusing interrogators of injecting a searing irritant into her sinus cavities and using other torture, which she did not elaborate on. And she repeated her insistence that she had no part in the murders. A spokesman for the Mexico City attorney general's office refused to comment on the allegations when contacted by the press.

Sara wasn't the only member of the gang who allegedly suffered the Mexican lawmen's wrath. "El Duby's" mysterious fall at police headquarters and swollen eye were viewed with suspicion by journalists and civil libertarians. Orea Ochoa chimed in with accusations that Federal Judicial Police had tortured him mentally and physically in efforts to force him to reveal the identities of famous and powerful Mexicans involved with the drug cultists. In Matamoros, both Sergio Martinez Salinas and Elio Hernandez Rivera also claimed they were tortured and forced to sign declarations linking them to the fifteen killings at the Santa Elena Ranch.

In Brownsville, city fathers were relieved to learn that the ringleaders of the killer cult were either dead or in police custody. Mayor Garza told reporters that rumors about where the gang would turn up next and about the possible kidnapping of children could at last be put to rest.

The mayor also had good words to say about how well law enforcement agencies in the United States and Mexico had worked together in the case. Cooperative efforts on both sides of the border had put the cult killers out of business, he said.

In the United States, news of Constanzo's death and Sara's arrest was greeted at the Kilroy home with grim resignation. The Kilroys had already buried their eldest son and were struggling to put Mark's horrifying death behind them.

"It doesn't strike me one way or another," James Kilroy told reporters from his home in Santa Fe, Texas, when informed that his son's alleged murderer had been killed by one of his own gang members during the gunbattle with police. He described Constanzo as a psychopathic killer whom law enforcement authorities were afraid would kill again.

"I bear no malice," he added. "But you can develop malice just by thinking about it again and again. When we buried Mark, we left (the investigation) up to George (Gavito). He wanted (Constanzo) bad. He said he was a deadly killer. For that reason, I'm glad they caught him."

CHAPTER 14

The Devil Didn't Die

WITHIN HOURS OF THE shootout in Mexico City, alarming rumors began to spread that Adolfo de Jesus Constanzo was not dead, and that he and his lover, Martin Quintana Rodriquez, had fled the apartment building during the height of the firefight and disappeared into Mexico City's criminal underground, leaving two look-alikes behind in their place.

Mexican police tried desperately to squelch the rumors the moment they began to surface, but even American investigators were skeptical that Constanzo, an intelligent and wily criminal mastermind, would order his own execution.

The two bloody bodies found in the apartment's spacious bedroom closet had been shot repeatedly in the head and chest, and identification was extremely difficult. Wasn't it possible, some police officials mused, that Constanzo had murdered two cult members that closely resembled he and Martin and hastily exited the hideout during the height of the frenzied gunbattle?

Adding credence to the rumors were reports in some Mexico City newspapers that two men were seen fleeing the scene of the shootout.

It made sense. After all, the gang had tried to throw police off their trail earlier by leaving behind specific items belonging to Sara Aldrete in the hope that investigators would believe she had been murdered by the ruthless cult because she knew too much about their activities. Some Mexican police were initially taken in by the effort to fake Sara's death, but most hard-bitten American cops refused to take the bait. Until Sara's body was found and definitively identified, they said at the time, they would continue to assume that the lanky cult godmother was still running with Constanzo and the gang. Their hunch was right — Sara was eventually captured alive and well.

DEA agent Armando Ramirez, stationed in Brownsville, was one of the first American investigators to voice suspicions that Constanzo may have faked his own death. "The guy's face is just about blown off," he told newsmen of the body discovered in the gang's Mexico City hideout. "You can dress somebody up with Constanzo's jewelry who is about the same size and make it look like him . . . I think there is a twist to this thing."

Cult member de Leon Valdez insisted at the time of his arrest that he had executed Constanzo and Quintana at the insistence of the Godfather himself, but American police, knowing the cult members' penchant for trickery and lies, weren't as quick as their Mexican counterparts to accept the story. While the bodies found in the apartment probably were those of the crazed cult leader and his homosexual lover, they wanted definitive proof in the form of fingerprint and dental comparisons.

"We are just saying it probably is him, but I wouldn't put it past (Constanzo) to get somebody to look like it was him that was killed, and to get his buddies and the broad (Sara), to go along with the story," Ramirez told Texas journalists.

Photos taken at the scene of the grisly suicide by execution showed that the body identified as Constanzo's was wearing no jewelry at the time of his death, and that although he was riddled with bullets from an Uzi, his features were fairly recognizable.

Mexican police categorically affirmed that the bodies were those of Constanzo and Quintana, noting that there was no reason to assume otherwise. A spokesman for the Mexico City attorney general stressed that Constanzo was identified by his own killer. His passport found near the body, and his features coincided with the passport photo and the picture on the police "wanted" bulletin, the spokesman added.

Nevertheless, rumors that Constanzo was still alive continued to spread throughout Mexico City.

Even some of the most respected and cautious newspapers in the United States reported the speculation that Constanzo and Quintana may have staged their own deaths in a last-ditch ploy to throw police off their trail once and for all.

Eager to put the whole incident behind them, American and Mexican police investigators met a few days after the shootout to compare Constanzo's fingerprints and dental charts, received from the U.S., with the remains. They matched! The devil and his lover were definitely dead, slain by multiple gunshot wounds to the head and abdomen. During autopsies, it was revealed that Constanzo had been shot fourteen times, and Quintana had been shot nineteen times. Both died instantly.

Police officials and residents of Matamoros and Mexico City breathed a collective sigh of relief. It had taken several grueling weeks of intensive, around-the-clock detective work to follow and locate the vicious cult leader, and even then the discovery of his final hideout had depended to a large extent on an incredible stroke of luck. But now there was no question that he was dead. *El Padrino*'s ungodly reign of terror had ended.

"When you get right down to it," Ramirez commented later to reporters, "Constanzo was a killer, he was a madman, and he proved it right up to the end. We had to be sure he was dead."

Despite the public hoopla surrounding Constanzo's death, members of his gang did not lose all hope at the news. They believed in reincarnation, police explained, and they simply took it for granted that Constanzo would return one day to continue his criminal ways. *El Padrino* would never truly die, they said. His body may have been destroyed, but his spirit lived on, waiting for the right moment to return to Earth and carry on the vile work he seemed destined by the gods to pursue.

Nevertheless, the legend of Adolfo de Jesus Constanzo, lives on.

In fact, Constanzo's gruesome and bloody acts in Matamoros have already inspired a ballad. Titled "Tragedy in Matamoros," it was written and performed by a Mexican-based group called Suspiros de Salamanca.

The ballad recounts the saga of Sara Aldrete and *El Padrino,* and details how their evil cult murdered innocent people — including Mark Kilroy, referred to in the song as a "young American" — to gain help from the devil in their smuggling endeavors. The song details how Mexican police stumbled on the horrifying murders at the Santa Elena Ranch when they captured one of the cult members.

Such ballads are called *corridos* in Spanish, and are commonly used in Mexico to tell about historical events or pressing social problems. "Tragedy in Matamoros." received strong air play in Mexico and several major Texas cities, including Houston and San Antonio, following the death of Constanzo.

The fact that Constanzo was bisexual and many members of his cult were homosexual added a bizarre twist to an already macabre case. Police fully realized the homosexual inclinations of the gang when they found several photographs in Constanzo's fashionable home in Mexico City showing the Godfather in relaxed, loving poses with various men — primarily Martin Quintana Rodriquez. Other photos gathered from Constanzo's homes by police were hard core homosexual pornography.

Quintana's sister later told police that her brother had a long-term relationship with Constanzo, whom he often referred to as his "boyfriend." In many of the photographs, Constanzo and Quintana were wearing matching outfits.

But Omar Orea Ochoa's photo and name also played a prominent part in documents and mementos the Godfather left behind, attesting to his enduring place in Constanzo's affections. A diary found in Constanzo's apartment indicated what police believed to be rankings of cult members. Listed right after Constanzo's name as *El Padrino,* Orea Ochoa's name appeared in the book as *Palero mayor,* which some investigators interpreted to mean he was the right-hand man. Sara was listed as *La Madrina,* and the names of other suspects were entered in the notebook as godchildren.

Another of Constanzo's journals recovered by police was filled with what he had identified as "recipes" for occult rituals, as well as the names of clients and homosexuals. One ritual called for five goats, five chickens and five cats as ingredients for a spell.

Constanzo never tried to hide his homosexuality. He seemed to prefer men who were almost mirror images of himself: handsome, smooth and nicely dressed. He treated his lovers well, showering them with generous gifts and writing passionate love letters and poems.

After Constanzo's body was autopsied, Mexico City authorities announced that if his family failed to make arrangements to claim the body within sixty days, it would be donated to a medical school for dissection. Constanzo's mother telephoned Sheriff Perez in Brownsville asking for advice to help her claim the body. U.S. consular officials eventually claimed the body on her behalf and had it flown to Miami.

Martin Quintana's body was claimed at Mexico City's central morgue by his brother after he and other family members were interrogated by police. Another man police talked to after questioning Quintana's survivors in the deputy attorney general's office told journalists that investigators suspected the gang in the murder of his wife two years earlier. With tears misting his eyes, he said that she vanished on May Day after leaving the Mexico City office where she worked as a secretary. Her mutilated body was discovered thirteen days later, with her stomach ripped out.

Constanzo's body was cremated, but other details of the funeral were kept secret because the family did not want the press or public intruding on their grief. Only family members and a handful of family friends were invited.

Earlier, Constanzo's brother, Fausto Rodriquez had told a Texas newspaper that he believed his brother had been falsely accused by vengeful gang members of killing the fifteen people in Matamoros. He speculated that there could be many reasons for the reputed frameup, including the possibility of revenge or envy.

Rodriquez also suggested that a "lover's quarrel" over the affections of Sara may have instigated a retaliation. He claimed that Sara fell in love with his brother and ignored other cult members, leading to the possibility of jealousy and revenge as motives for a frameup.

Constanzo's loyal brother also refused to accept stories that Adolfo was involved in sacrificial murder. He said his brother attended Catholic Church and Catholic schools, and would not have become involved with human sacrifice. Constanzo's fourteen-year-old sister also described Adolfo as a loving brother.

During a search of one of the cult leader's homes in Mexico City, Police found Constanzo's will, which he had written in January 1989.

"This is my will," the document read. "If I die, my properties and cars will belong to Martin (Quintana Rodriquez) and Omar (Orea Ochoa). The apartment and everything inside I leave to Omar, the house and everything inside to Martin. Sell the Mercedes, and split the money equally between Rodriquez and Ochoa. The same with the Lincoln town car. The money will be split in two parts, one for Martin and the other for Omar. Also, the money I have in the house will be divided in two parts, one for Rodriquez, the other for Ochoa. My jewelry also will be divided between Omar and Martin. These are my only inheritables. Martin was born Dec. 9, 1964, and Omar born Oct. 22, 1965. (signed) Adolfo de Jesus Constanzo."

It took a Mexican handwriting expert nearly ten days to verify that the signature on the document was Constanzo's.

After the shootout in Mexico City and the apprehension of Sara and other cult members, police investigators began retracing the gang's days on the run.

Sara told police that she had originally planned to leave the Rio Grande Valley on the morning of April 10 for a holiday in Mexico City, but had difficulty getting a visa and instead left that evening. It was the night before the discovery at the Santa Elena Ranch.

While piecing together the escape route, investigators confirmed that the gang members split up before leaving Brownsville. Constanzo, de Leon and at least one other male gang member flew together, probably from McAllen, Texas, to Mexico City. Sara booked a separate flight and flew to Mexico City where she was met by a female associate of Constanzo's who took her to his elegant residence in suburban Antizapan de Zaragoza.

Police also checked into reports that Constanzo and two or three of his male companions flew from Mexico City to Miami. Investigators, however, indicated that Constanzo, Sara and the others spent the entire twenty-five days between the grim discovery at the Santa Elena Ranch and the shootout, moving from one location to another in the Mexico City area.

But the reports of a side trip to Miami helped fuel suspicions that Constanzo had stashed a large cache of money there. His relatives, however, insisted that they knew of no secret bank accounts or other caches of cash.

Instead of fleeing to Miami when he learned that police were hot on his trail, Constanzo telephoned a former fashion model he had once performed a *limpia* for. He asked Maria del Rocio Cuevas Guerra for help finding a hideout. Immediately after her arrest she had been presented to the press as somewhat of a mystery woman, known by her nickname, Carla. According to her account, which she later related to police, she at first refused to help. But after Constanzo telephoned her again and threatened to kill her family, she agreed to find him a place to hide out.

She told police that she was afraid that he would eventually be captured, do some prison time, then win release and track her down and murder her if she didn't help. So she located an apartment for him through the want ads in a local newspaper. He didn't stay there long.

As police reassembled *El Padrino*'s escape route, they traced him and as many as eight other suspects at various times, from his apartment to a property just outside the Federal District, and to a remote cabin near the famous volcano, Popocatepetl, which looms across Mexico City's southeastern horizon, before the gang finally settled into the fourth-floor apartment near the center of the capital where they were finally found.

While police were closing in on the fugitives, raiding Constanzo's apartments and a house — at least once, only a few hours after their quarry had cleared out — the discovery of two altars confirmed the Godfather's dependence on dark forces. One of the altars was found in the home in Antizapan de Zaragoza, and the other in one of the Mexico City apartments. Both were similar to the altar found at the Santa Elena Ranch. One of the homes was outfitted with a satellite dish, which sparked stories in the Mexican press that it was installed to capture pornographic films for use during demonic orgies.

After the shootout, Sara claimed she didn't learn about the murders at the gang's Matamoros hideaway until the night following her flight from the border, as she and Constanzo were watching television in his Mexico City apartment.

In statements to police and the press she said that as news of the discovery at the ranch was flashed on the screen, Constanzo exclaimed: "They found them!"

Her startled response, according to her story, was, "They found what?"

Sara said it wasn't until then that Constanzo told her the whole sordid tale of kidnap, mutilation, and murder.

Sara's family was relieved by the news that their daughter was in police custody, and not dead as many people believed. "God took care of her for us," Sara's father, Israel Aldrete, told reporters.

Her parents said that now they knew she was alive and safe and healthy, they would be able to rest easier. They had not heard from their daughter for several weeks and were worried that Constanzo had murdered her to keep her from talking about the cult's bloody activities.

The couple said they believed their daughter's tearful claims to police and reporters that she had nothing to do with the ritual slayings at the ranch. They confirmed that they would stand by her and do everything they could to help her.

They said they were surprised when police searching Sara's bedroom found the altar and splattered blood.

Sara insisted in her statements to the press that the altar and accoutrements found in her Matamoros bedroom were Christian icons, not Satanic objects. "They were saints — Saint Francis of Assisi, Saint Barbara, Santo Nino de Atocho — the guardian angel of Constanzo," she declared.

It was an old story that cult experts, and long ago, slave owners and Christian missionaries, had heard before. The religious personalities of Christian saints were deliberately merged with more sinister African gods to disguise their true identities from suspicious outsiders.

Even though Constanzo was dead and core cult members apprehended, the investigation into the cult's activities continued to grow as new suspects were identified and warrants issued for their arrest.

Police picked up Enrique Calzada, the alleged boyfriend of "Carla," shortly after the shootout.

Constanzo had been known among Mexico City's rich, famous and powerful, as a person who could turn their luck around — for a price, investigators learned. Among the several well-known personalities named by the cultists or in the Mexico City press as believed to be former clients or associates of the infamous *brujo* were spitfire actress and vocalist Irma Serrano, celebrity hairstylist Afredo Palacios, singer Oscar Athie, singer and soap opera star Lucia Mendez, and female pop singer Yuri. All adamantly denied having any connection with Constanzo's criminal or cult activities.

Miss Serrano, who is probably as well known in Mexico for her role as the one-time troublesome mistress of former President Gustavo Diaz Ordaz as for her acting and singing abilities, told the press that she was not involved in Constanzo's diabolical cult activities.

The actress, who wears a diamond mounted in a front tooth and paints her eyebrows in a high arch that resembles those of "Star Trek's" Mr. Spock, is called *La Tigresa*, (The Tigress) by her fans and delighted gossip columnists. She said she had never attended rituals conducted by the cultists. But she boldly admitted that she would have been interested in an invitation.

"Yes, I love Satan," she told reporters. "But I wasn't involved in any drugs or killing or eating people. I'm interested in Satan worship, so if these people had invited me to their temple, I would have gone. But they didn't."

Athie seemed to be more shaken. And Palacios was less accessible to the media.

As police began to wind down their investigation of Constanzo and his blood-drenched gang, concern grew over reports that the cult had splintered and smaller groups existed in Mexico and the United States.

Investigation failed to produce any solid evidence to back up the fears, but it worried authorities nonetheless. Constanzo had made a lot of connections during his reign of terror, and it was not inconceivable that followers unknown to police were planning to continue in his demonic footsteps.

In Matamoros, Commandante Benitez Ayala told the press that he was hopeful that no similar sects were operating as Constanzo's cultists did. But the possibility couldn't be ignored that spinoffs from a network of cultists may have been left behind.

Police in San Antonio considered the possibility of a breakaway group of cultists surviving the Matamoros-Mexico City gang after reviewing the activities of an alleged ring of Cuban-led drug smugglers who were practicing what appeared to be a twisted form of *Santeria*. Broken up earlier in the year, the reputed gang was being investigated in connection with twelve murders in the San Antonio area since 1985. There were subtle indications that the group might be connected in some way to Constanzo's gang — foremost being the fact that both groups are headed by Cubans — but a subsequent investigation failed to turn up definitive connection between the two organizations.

And the omnipresence of dark cult activity continued to prove itself in the U.S. as federal DEA agents swooped down on a home in the San Francisco Bay area and discovered a sacrificial altar, animal organs, a human skull and a human spinal cord — all apparently used in rituals similar to those performed by Constanzo and his followers.

A DEA group supervisor said six suspects arrested at the home may have been practicing *Palo Mayombe* or *Santeria* to obtain protection for a reputed cocaine smuggling operation. All the suspects were of Colombian or Cuban origin.

But unlike Constanzo, who personally killed the men selected for his unholy religious ceremonies, the accused drug runners in California were not suspected of homicide, police officials said — although it was not completely ruled out.

Constanzo and his minions had clearly forever branded into the public consciousness an awareness and fear of blood cults. He died, but his spirit and the evil he inflicted seem certain to live on.

CHAPTER 15

Slaughter in Mexico City

NO ONE INDIVIDUAL REALLY knows how many deaths Constanzo and his depraved minions may be responsible for — but it appears likely that the total is closer to thirty than the fifteen of which they are accused in Matamoros.

Investigators for law enforcement agencies have determined that *El Padrino* probably began his blood purge in Mexico City at least eighteen months before moving to the border towns of Matamoros and Brownsville. But pinning down the exact number of men and women whose lives actually ended violently, either by Constanzo's own hand, or at his direction, is difficult.

Police in Mexico are no different than those in the United States in their wish to clear up unsolved crimes, especially murders, and in particular those that are unusually grisly or which seem to have cult connections.

Only a few years before the slaughter in Matamoros and Mexico City engineered by Constanzo, a one-eyed, bisexual drifter named Henry Lee Lucas was, for a brief period, the most celebrated criminal in the world. Lucas confessed to committing more than 360 murders, while roaming thirty-six states, raping, robbing, and butchering relatives, friends, and strangers.

Elated police prepared to close the books on hundreds of unsolved murders, including several in Texas, before Lucas shifted gears and began recanting his dramatic confessions. He decided that he had committed only three murders, including the slaying of his alcoholic mother. Embarrassed lawmen began reluctantly admitting that they had been mistaken about some of the cases so suddenly solved, and reopened scores of investigations. Lucas was eventually convicted of ten slayings, and is currently on death row in the Texas State Penitentiary at Huntsville.

But there is a lesson to be learned. Serial killers, when they are at last exposed, offer an almost irresistible opportunity for frustrated police officers to close the books on every troublesome case that may have even the slightest resemblance to the suspect's modus operandi.

So it should have been no surprise, when barely three months after

Mark Kilroy's mutilated remains were exhumed from his shallow grave at the Santa Elena Ranch, that law enforcement authorities had linked the Constanzo gang to about twenty additional killings in the Mexico City area. Undoubtedly some, although probably not all, of the slayings being so rapidly tied to Constanzo and his cohorts, were indeed their diabolical handiwork.

For weeks the Mexico City news media printed and broadcast stories heralding new horrors thought to be linked to the gang. It seemed that there was no hair-raising atrocity that the cultists weren't capable of, and hadn't committed as a result of their formidable marriage of drug smuggling, black magic, and ritual murder.

Even in Matamoros, 550 miles north of the capital, Commandante Benitez Ayala told the press that there were "a lot of murders" in Mexico City's Colonia Roma area that were connected to Constanzo.

Some of the slayings were classic gangland rubouts. Others carried the unmistakable mark of human sacrifice, or cult slayings. And at least one, that of the unfortunate La Claudia, appeared to be nothing more than a personal quarrel involving neither drugs nor religious ritual.

La Claudia's brutal slaying may have been the murder that first whetted his tastebuds for the warm flavor and aroma of blood, and altered his psyche to the heady feeling of power that for some is said to accompany the act of deliberate homicide. Once *El Padrino*'s blood lust had been awakened, he killed often, and with malicious delight. The prospects of survival for anyone unfortunate enough to offend him were fragile.

There is no question that the luckless cross-dresser, who also used the names Omar and Ramon Baez was found dismembered and dumped in the Zumpango River. Police accused three of Constanzo's reputed associates of participating with the Godfather in the slaying.

Mexican Federal Judicial Police quoted the ex-fashion model known as "Carla" as stating after her arrest following the shootout at the apartment on Rio Sena, that she had introduced Constanzo to a transvestite who was eventually beheaded during a ritual murder.

And investigators determined that at least one other cross-dressing homosexual in addition to La Claudia, was probably killed in Mexico City by the Constanzo-led gangsters. The victim, known as Claudio Yvonne, was mutilated and dismembered in 1987.

Orea Ochoa told reporters at one of the press conferences a few hours after his arrest that he helped *El Padrino* pick up a transvestite in the Pink Zone, and take the unsuspecting victim to a nearby apartment. But there has been some confusion and disagreement about just how the murder took place.

Some Mexico City police and journalists privately refer to the case as "the wishbone slaying." They believe that the shrieking transvestite was tied to two cars — one leg fastened to the rear bumper of each of the vehicles — which then took off in opposite directions, accomplishing instant dismemberment and death.

But other accounts indicate that the homosexual was killed in the apartment, chopped into pieces, stuffed in plastic garbage bags and loaded into the trunk of Constanzo's silver-colored Lincoln and disposed of. Orea Ochoa said that the Godfather removed the spine of his victim to use as a good luck necklace.

Neighbors who lived near one of the houses in the suburbs frequented by Constanzo and his gang, sometimes discussed among themselves the curious necklaces of garlic cloves that he and the other young men wore. The discussions would later center on the nauseating suspicions that the necklaces may not have been made of garlic cloves after all, but were human vertebrae ripped from the bodies of the gang's butchered victims in disgusting acts of necrophilic madness.

The same neighbors recoiled in horror when police reported finding blood splattered altars in some of the homes inhabited by the gang, and writers and columnists in Mexican newspapers began speculating that newborn human babies, possibly bred specifically for use in demonic blood rites, had been sacrificed.

One of the cult suspects told authorities that after La Claudia was murdered and dismembered, Constanzo ordered him to leave and return with a baby because he needed more blood for a ritual. He claimed that he never delivered the baby, but his account of La Claudia's death was chilling. He said that the transvestite was fighting furiously for his life, so Constanzo ordered his hands and legs securely bound. Then Constanzo pulled a plastic bag over La Claudia's head and suffocated him. Finally, the Godfather cut his victim's throat with a knife, and followed up by chopping off the arms and legs.

Fueled by stories like the account of the aftermath of the transvestite killing, the chilling rumors of baby sacrifice persisted, but law enforcement authorities have continued to insist that the reports are untrue. The crimes attributed to Constanzo's drug cultists were horrible enough, without infanticide. But it seemed there was no end to the horror they had set in motion in Mexico and the United States.

Juan Miguel Ponce, an FJP inspector general in Mexico City attempted to down play the homosexual element in the atrocities committed by Constanzo and his followers. In a statement to the press he said *El Padrino*'s homosexual behavior had only a minor role in his criminal activities. The important link between Constanzo and his criminal band was their belief in *Palo Mayombe*, Ponce declared.

"It's like being blonde or thin or fat. The relation was with the witchery, not their sexual preference," the FJP official insisted.

It was true that a disproportionate number of the murders Constanzo and his gang were suspected of carried unmistakable signs of human sacrifice. Among additional ritual-like killings investigators were seeking to link the Constanzo gang to were the deaths of five men and three women whose mutilated bodies were found weighted with cement blocks and the lids of heavy iron cauldrons in the warm waters of a lake just outside the capital city. Police recovered the bodies of the lake victims following a tip that a housekeeper had vanished after telling friends that she was going somewhere to attend a black mass. The chests of each of the victims had been slashed open. Some had suffered various other forms of mutilation as well, including severing of the fingertips — the classic mark left by Mexican drug trade executioners to indicate the elimination of informers.

A senior investigator with a team of more than fifteen lawmen investigating the case, stated that the murders were definitely linked to Constanzo. The method of operation used in the lake killings, and slayings already definitely known to have been committed by the deadly mystic with the diabolical quicksilver mind, was the same.

The drug cultists were also named as suspects in the dismemberment slayings of three other men whose remains were found floating in the Zumpango during 1987 and early 1988.

The ritualistic murder of a man found a few days later lying in a municipal park with his legs extending straight down from his body and his arms thrust out at the sides in the shape of a cross, was added to the list of killings being probed by police for possible connection to Constanzo's cultists. The corpse was surrounded with a circle of rocks, and the slaying had all the appearances of human sacrifice by a blood cult.

A veteran homicide officer said that he and his colleagues were baffled for months by the eerie case, until they learned of the Matamoros homicides and made a possible connection between the crimes.

Other lawmen in Mexico City have indicated the body count of cult victims is likely to increase dramatically as the investigation of Constanzo's activities since first coming to the capital continues to develop. Some are convinced that Constanzo initiates have formed separate circles of cultists who are still carrying on his diabolical work.

A highly placed investigator said that as new members were attracted, Constanzo is believed to have initiated outstanding acolytes as godfathers and godmothers and charged them with the authority and responsibility to train recruits and establish new branches of the cult.

Spokesmen for the Mexico City attorney general's office revealed, early in the investigation, that Sara Aldrete confirmed to investigators that Constanzo had followers in South Florida who were schooled in his religious teachings and rituals. And Miami is notorious as a hotbed of both cult and drug trafficking murders. Mutilated bodies, sometimes without heads, are found there dumped in rivers, canals and the bay. Others have been disposed of in municipal parks or vacant lots, uniquely mutilated, or with stones, shells and beads arranged around them in a ritualistic manner.

Prisons and morgues in the Miami area have also yielded intriguing clues to the exotic marks branded on the shoulders and arms of some of Constanzo's most favored followers. After the mass migration to the United States of Cuban criminals and lunatics released by Castro from prisons and madhouses during the Carter Administration, jailers and morgue attendants began noticing strange tattoos. DEA officials in Miami eventually began a study of the marks, and learned that many of them represented spirit deities of the Afro-Caribbean religions of *Santaria* and *Palo Mayombe,* and a substantial number of the tattoos identified crime specialties as well. The criminals, and non-criminals who have unfortunately been branded in the press and the public mind with the same reputation as their dishonest brethren, left Cuba at the port of Mariel, and are commonly referred to as *Marielitos.*

The symbols worn by the criminal *Marielitos* helped establish a pecking order on the street and in prison, and were usually, although not always inscribed on the skin flap between the thumb and forefinger. The symbol for executioner — the professional killers or hit men of the gangs — was a heart pierced by an arrow, with the word, *madre,* mother. Elio Hernandez Rivera and Alvero de Leon Valdez, *El Duby,* carried arrow marks branded on their bodies by Constanzo, that reputedly signified their exalted positions in the cult hierarchy as executioner priests. *El Padrino* himself bore an arrow-shaped self-inflicted scar on one of his shoulders. He said it was a sign that he had been chosen by the gods to kill.

Among the criminal *Marielitos,* drug dealers were identified by a verticle-shaped line with two others slightly slanted, one on each side, and two verticle lines at the bottom. Enforcers were marked with an upended trident.

Charts illustrating the unique shapes of the telltale tattoos and their significance were distributed to police agencies throughout Dade county (Miami).

But the *Marielitos,* who include some of the most desperate and vicious criminals produced in Cuba, have spread throughout the U.S. and the rest of the Western Hemisphere and are known to be heavily involved in the international drug trade and other criminal pursuits. And they took their fearlessness, savagery, and blood cults with them, although Constanzo was not a *Marielito,* and indeed was born in the United States.

Investigations by Mexico City police have tied him to the brazen execution of almost an entire drug-smuggling family gang during a dramatic shootout with machine guns on the violence-ridden capital's Barcelona Street. Nine members of the Calzada family were mowed down in the street-corner bloodbath. The killers then scooped up the bodies of their victims and threw them in the Tula River.

Despite the brazen nature of the 1987 massacre, the case was unsolved and police were left without sufficient evidence to make an arrest until Sara and some of her companions behind bars, began talking about it. They reportedly claimed in statements to investigators that Salvador Vidal Garcia Alarcon, a Mexican federal narcotics agent joined with Constanzo, Quintana, and other cultists to carry out the slayings. The thirty-nine-year-old Alarcon, a career police officer denied any involvement with the murders, and claimed his ties to the sect were limited solely to its occultism.

The Calzadas were reportedly killed because they had evidence of police involvement in the cult's drug trafficking activities.

The probe of Constanzo's criminal activities in Mexico City and along the border, has turned up increasing evidence that he worked closely with larger, well-organized and financed gangs in other countries.

The U.S. Customs enforcement division is among agencies known to be probing the possibility that he had ties to the Chicago Mob, or other criminal organizations in the Windy City. And before the death of Saul Hernandez, it was known that he had links to American gangsters in the Midwest capable of handling large shipments of narcotics. Considering Constanzo's fierce business and criminal savvy, it seems inconceivable that he would not have maintained and broadened similar ties.

About two weeks after the death of Constanzo, authorities announced the arrest of Salvador Vidal Garcia Alarcon, a federal narcotics agent, on drug trafficking charges. He was accused of being Constanzo's companion in the raid on the dentist's office in Guadalajara and theft of the cocaine. The thirty-nine-year-old policeman pleaded innocent to the charges, and told authorities that his involvement with the cult was limited to witchcraft and had nothing to do with drug trafficking or murder. Sara told investigators that when she first met Garcia Vidal, Constanzo introduced him to her as one of his godchildren.

Other gang members already in custody, identified him as a cult priest, and claimed that several other federal police officers had become involved in their criminal activities.

A spokesman for the Attorney General's Office claimed, however, that Vidal Garcia was the only federal agent involved in the crimes committed by members of the sect. "We are cleaning house," he said.

Suspects of the gang

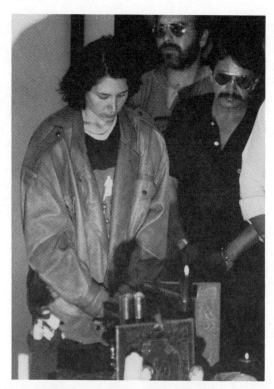

Sara pleading her innocence.

Press conference of the suspects.

CHAPTER 16

The Case Against the Devil's Children

AFTER THE FIRST OUTRAGED flurry of calls for extradition of the accused cult killers to the United States so that they could be made to face Texas justice, law officers, court officials and politicians publicly and privately agreed to the obvious.

Since the murders and most of the other crimes the suspects were accused of occurred in Mexico, it was legally and ethically appropriate that they should face trial there.

"It's a Mexican show," a U.S. Embassy spokesman in Mexico City said.

Talking with reporters, the embassy official flatly turned thumbs down on the possibility that any efforts might be made to extradite the suspects to face drug trafficking and other lesser charges in American courts after Mexican authorities have settled with them. He pointed out that in comparison with the grisly killings in Matamoros and Mexico City, any crimes they were accused of in the United States were relatively minor.

Some U.S. law enforcement officers, including Lieutenant Gavito and Customs Agent Oran Neck, were invited to Mexico City to assist in the investigation, however.

The five suspects arrested at the scene of the shootout were initially booked on charges of homicide, criminal association, wounding a police agent, and damage to property.

As police officers kept the pressure on seeking out suspected gang members who escaped the roundup of accused cultists at the mid-town apartment, interrogators focused much of their questioning on efforts aimed at determining if the prisoners were involved in any federal crimes. But whether or not federal crimes could be proven to have occurred, it appeared certain that the defendants would be put on trial in federal courts because of the highly centralized form of government in Mexico which traditionally moves many cases there from state courts.

After a few hours in custody, the exhausted suspects were arraigned in night-time proceedings, hastily arranged to expedite the case as well as to avoid the horde of reporters and photographers who had descended on the city from all over the world. They pleaded innocent to the charges, including the most serious — first degree homicide — lodged against *El Duby* and Sara, in the deaths of Constanzo and Quintana.

Ochoa joined Sara in claiming they were held against their will when the gang went underground in Mexico City after the horror in Matamoros was uncovered. Orea Ochoa said his former lover and five-year companion threatened him with death.

Despite Orea Ochoa's and Sara's pleas, the court ruled that there was sufficient evidence against them and their companion, de Leon Valdez, to warrant a trial. All three were ordered held without bond.

The decision about bail was tied to a formula which provides for the court to add up the minimum and maximum penalties for the charges against defendants, then divide by two. If the total is less than five years, bail can be granted. If it is five years or more, no bail is allowed.

Despite the seriousness of the crimes the trio of cultists were reputedly involved in, they faced prison time if convicted of no more than fifty years each. Fifty years is the maximum according to Mexican law, which does not permit stacking penalties to pile up sentences of hundreds of thousands of years. And Mexico has no death penalty.

Whatever the outcome in court of Sara and Ochoa's claims of innocence, they were certain to remain in jail, probably for a year or more, even if eventually found not guilty. But there would be no frustrating or seemingly endless delays, such as those that so hopelessly gridlock criminal courts in the U.S. Experienced court watchers in Mexico City estimated that the charges against the accused cultists would be disposed of no later than the summer or fall of 1990.

According to Mexican law after a judge has decided that evidence against a suspect warrants a trial, he basically has one year to collect and examine documents from the prosecution and defense before sentencing defendants or finding them not guilty.

The Civil Code, which follows Napoleonic law adopted in Mexico in the early nineteenth century, allows prosecutors and the courts to proceed with the presumption that defendants are guilty. Unlike American criminal law, which presumes the defendant to be innocent until proven guilty, in Mexico defendants must prove themselves innocent.

In Mexico, documents play an important role in the judicial system. In the U.S., tedious pretrial hearings can drag almost endlessly with lawyers haranguing judges on fine points of law for months before a case is ready to be heard by a jury or before the bench.

Mexico also has pretrial proceeding, but very little live testimony is allowed. Most of the information developed for the proceeding is spelled out in documents, including depositions from witnesses, police and defendants.

There is no place for courtroom histrionics, no provision for impassioned speeches before bored jurors by the prosecutor or by strutting defense lawyers. In Mexico the courts conduct what are basically office trials, where arguments for and against defendants are produced in writing.

Undoubtedly the most dramatic and obvious difference in U.S. and Mexican law is the absence of juries. The Mexican legal system does not provide for juries. Cases are decided by judges after digesting the mounds of documents collected by lawyers and prosecutors.

Following arraignment of the prisoners in Mexico City, they were transferred from the Miguel Hidalgo district police station on the capital's west side to more secure quarters at the Reclusorio Oriente Penitentiary. The austere prison considered to be one of Mexico's toughest and most secure prisons, which holds some of Mexico's most desperate criminals, is located at the eastern edge of the city.

The suspected cultists were moved there not only to prevent the possibility of escape or a breakout engineered by confederates on the outside, but to protect them from other inmates as well.

A highly placed Mexican court official cautioned that the press conferences had exposed the suspects to major risk of assassination, either by fearful cultists still at large, or more likely, by rival drug dealers.

Constanzo built his short-lived crime empire partly on his ability to rip-off other drug traffickers, and to eliminate competition by the most ruthless and hideous methods possible. It seemed reasonable to believe that at least some of the survivors of his deadly program were in the same prison as the cultists and would take any opportunity for revenge.

There was also the added fear that the surviving cultists would provide law enforcement agencies with valuable information about the identity and drug dealing methods of other gangs, possibly as tradeoffs for lighter sentences or special privileges. Constanzo, and his gang, presumably gathered information about drug dealers for which he had provided psychic counseling and protection, even if they didn't work together on smuggling activities.

Every drug dealer around wants to kill them, lawmen warned. The dealers are afraid of them, and they hate them. They know too much.

Spokesmen for the prosecutor's office and other arms of the legal justice system, however, credited the high-profile case and the firestorm of international interest it generated from the press, as helping with the investigation.

The back-to-back news conferences with the suspects on the two days following the wild-west style shootout in the heart of the city, had raised public awareness of cult-like practices all over the capital. Police agencies registered hundreds of telephone tips from citizens about sinister appearing activities by their neighbors. Other callers tipped off police about suspicious disappearances of acquaintances or family members, that helped in the probe.

Finally, the spokesmen said, the suspects appeared to talk more openly to reporters at the press conferences and to reveal details that they hadn't disclosed during police interrogations. "They seem to be more candid when they speak to the press than when they talk with us. When they are in front of the cameras, it makes them feel important, and they talk freely," he remarked.

Sara provided a good example of the relaxed attitude most of the suspects seemed to take when meeting the press. Before getting to the point and replying to reporters' questions about her possible involvement in cult killings, she chattered on-and-on in Spanish at one of the press conferences about the good grades she got at school and her desire to become a doctor.

With their cases involving the alleged Mexico City crimes already moving swiftly through the courts, early in June, Sara, de Leon Valdez and Ochoa were arraigned in the 9th Federal Criminal Court in the capital on a variety of charges tied to the Matamoros slayings and border drug running.

As she did when questioned about the Mexico City murders, Sara denied she had anything to do with the border slayings. But Gavito, in an interview on "The Reporters," insisted that he had evidence she was present when people were tortured at the ranch. He cited people already behind bars, as well as another individual who was present at the ranch but wasn't arrested as providing him with information about her involvement.

He said he was convinced that she was involved in eighty percent of the slayings at the ranch. He added that she had made telephone calls in which she discussed the sacrifice of Mark Kilroy, and said she knew exactly why Constanzo wanted the fairhaired young student: for his brain.

The most serious charges against Sara were related to the slayings of Constanzo and Quintana, and of the Mexico City transvestite, Omar Baez, also know as Rafael Paz Esquival and *La Claudia*.

She was accused of homicide in the slayings of the godfather and his lover after signing a confession admitting that she told de Leon Valdez just before police bulled their way into the apartment, to "get it over with" and shoot the homosexual lovers.

A spokesman for the Mexico City attorney general's office explained that Sara and Orea Ochoa were charged in the Constanzo-Quintana shootings because they had agreed to a death pact by the lovers in case arrest appeared to be imminent. And that pact was carried out.

Although she did not actually pull the trigger, "she incited the other man to do it and that makes her guilty of homicide," a spokesman for the Mexico City Attorney's office explained.

He added that prosecutors were seeking the gravest penalties available through Mexico's criminal justice system, fifty years in prison.

Later, in the conflicting confessions, retractions, statements at press conferences and private media interviews by the accused cultists, Sara claimed she never admitted yelling at de Leon Valdez to shoot the Godfather and his lover. She said police added the statement that she screamed the order to *El Duby*, before making her sign the declaration.

She told the press during various appearances and interviews that instead, she was yelling for her companions to stop shooting.

Police, prosecutors, and journalists were being faced with an increasingly difficult task of piecing together the welter of names, nicknames, aliases, and conflicting statements from Sara and the other suspects into an understandable chronology. Many of the wild and wooly press accounts filed by Mexican journalists solved the problem the easy way. They simply left attributions for statements, locations, and times out of their stories. But police, prosecutors, defense attorneys, judges, and others in the criminal justice system had no such easy escape chute to depend on. Somehow they would have to assemble the perplexing crazy quilt of facts, accusations and confessions into a coherent account of the gang's criminal activities in Mexico City and on the border.

Signs of tension between some of the suspects began to emerge when de Leon told police that the only members of the gang really deeply into black magic were Constanzo and his two favorite lovers, Quintata and Orea Ochoa. De Leon added that the baby-faced Orea Ochoa was not the "white dove" he was pretending to be, but a skilled occultist who knew more about black magic than even the *Padrino*.

Sara was also bending under the strain. She was beginning to show the physical and emotional effects of her incarceration and ordeal with the fugitive gang. She was rapidly losing her looks and charm. Deprived of most cosmetics, and with her frightened eyes filled with tears, her nose appeared more prominent, somehow too big for her face. And when she talked, her mouth hung slack, wet and loose. The luster was gone from her brown hair, and it hung tiredly onto her shoulders.

When Lieutenant Gavito, who had watched the pathetic remains of the cult's victims pulled from the fetid graves at the Santa Elena Ranch, was asked on "The Reporters," if he believed her claims of abuse at the hands of the police, he replied: "I don't know. But if she was tortured, it's the best thing that ever happened to her. I don't think she was tortured enough."

The shooting of Constanzo and Quintana weren't the only slayings Sara and Orea Ochoa were accused of involvement in. Authorities also charged her with criminal association and with obstructing justice by helping to cover up the ritual mutilation and murder of Ramon Baez, *La Claudia*, in Mexico

City the summer before the discovery in Matamoros sent the gang underground.

Sara said she didn't witness *La Claudia*'s murder, and she didn't report it to police because when the Godfather told her about it, she thought he was merely trying to impress her with a made-up story.

But Orea and two other men arrested in Mexico City after the shootout, were also named with her in charges related to the transsexual's slaying. Juan Carlos Fragoso and Salvador Antonio Gutierrez Juarez, also known as Jorge Montes, were each imprisoned without bail by a federal judge because of the severity of the charges. Police said Gutierrez Juarez confessed to helping Constanzo kill *La Claudia*. The three men were charged with homicide, and with violating burial laws by dumping the body in the river.

Family members of most of the suspects were permitted to attend the arraignment for the Constanzo and Quintana slayings, and waited patiently in a federal courtroom from 10:00 A.M., until 3:30 P.M. when the proceedings at last began. Sara's heartbroken father had travelled from Matamoros, bringing her fresh clothing, a blanket and personal grooming items before the arraignment.

At one point in the brief proceedings, Orea Ochoa's mother and three brothers, and two brothers of de Leon Valdez approached the barred area of the courtroom where the prisoners were kept and signalled their love and God's blessings before they were ushered away by court officials.

The defendants were directed to respond to statements in transcripts prepared after their interrogation by investigators, either concurring, making denials, making corrections, or adding information they claimed had been left out.

Sara conceded in her statement that she had practiced *Santaria*, but described it as *Christian Santeria*, which she insisted did not include human sacrifice.

However, she also admitted attending ceremonies during which animals were ritually slain and sacrificed. She said she was blindfolded during one of the ceremonies, but could hear chickens and the bleat of a goat as their throats were slit.

Appearing weary, dressed in a shapeless beige prison uniform, Sara once broke into tears when her father's name was brought up during a brief talk with her lawyer after she had been questioned about the transcripts. "I want to see my father," she sobbed.

Another reputed cultist said to have been recruited from Mexico City's tawdry homosexual underground, was initially suspected in the slaying of *La Claudia*, but was cleared of any involvement. A prosecutor remarked that the only crime the man had committed in relation to *La Claudia* was being the last person to sleep with the transvestite.

The cultist was retained in custody however, on other charges for alleg-edly killing David Rivera, another homosexual he allegedly had a sexual re-lationship with. The prisoner was accused of fatally stabbing Rivera after quarrelling over a romantic rival.

Following court appearances a few days after the shootout, Dr. Maria de Lourdes Guero Lopez, who was also known as "Klara," and "Carla," the bad-luck plagued model, were freed on high bail, to await resolution of the charges against them for allegedly helping the fugitives. There was also talk of filing possible charges of helping cover-up the Matamoros murders, a fed-eral crime. Dr. de Lourdes Guero Lopez, who allegedly offered some medical assistance to the fugitives, was quoted in the Mexican press as saying that when she learned the truth about the gang's activities she tried to leave. But Constanzo threatened to harm her family and to sacrifice her in a ritual.

Jose Enrique Calzada, Carla's boyfriend, who was accused of helping Constanzo find the cabin hideout near Popocatepetl and a downtown apart-ment, as well as exchanging American dollars for pesos, was also released on bail.

In Matamoros, the Public Ministry petitioned the federal courts for ex-tradition of de Leon Valdez, Orea Ochoa, and Sara to face trial for drug traf-ficking and homicide — crimes linked to the slaughter at the Santa Elena Ranch. The prisoners were formally notified of the additional charges by a federal court judge in Mexico City.

Mexican judicial authorities were also moving rapidly with the cases against the accused cultists arrested in Matamoros. The quartet, Elio Her-nandez Rivera, David Serna Valdez, Sergio Martinez Salinas and Serafin Hernandez Garcia, were locked up in the Tamaulipas State Prison in Mata-moros without bail on multiple charges tied to the ranch slayings and drug running.

Among the various counts they faced were homicide, kidnapping, viola-tion of firearms regulations, criminal association, crimes against the public health, weapons smuggling, and posing as police officers. No single suspect was charged with all of the violations, and only Hernandez Rivera was ac-cused of murder. But most of the charges were serious enough that conviction on even one count would assure the maximum penalty provided by the Mex-ican penal code.

Like their counterparts in Mexico City, the prisoners were held under heavy guard in maximum security cells for their own protection as much as to prevent possible escape. Commandante Benitez Ayala and others respon-sible for their safety and prosecution, was determined that the prisoners would live to face trial.

Six Matamoros Security Police squad cars escorted a van that carried the suspects from their jail cells to court for their arraignment in a closely guarded room on the second floor of the court building. Uniformed officers with riot guns surrounded the structure, and both sides of the street were blocked off to traffic.

As evidence to be presented at the arraignment, the prosecution had collected small amounts of marijuana and cocaine, a 9mm pistol, a 9mm automatic assault rifle, photos and other items.

Court authorities read from a stack of 550 papers collected for the arraignment, and the prosecutor questioned the suspects for more than three hours. The prosecutor's words were chilling in the direct simplicity of his recitation. He talked of Mark's kidnapping, about the telephone call to Constanzo at the motel, and about the Texas student's savage murder.

"The Godfather said he needed a young man?" the prosecutor asked at one point. Continuing a bit later, he stated, "You had him tied up in a warehouse where everyone met. The Godfather went in with Elio while the rest remained outside for fifteen minutes before a loud noise was heard like a coconut being split."

One-at-a-time, the prosecutor repeated his grisly descriptions of the murders, detailing each slaying with grim intensity. Never once did the sullen-faced suspects exhibit any emotion or speak up to confirm or deny his statements.

A court official later explained to reporters that they refused to respond because they did not have an attorney present at the hearing. They turned down representation by a municipal attorney who was assigned to the case. As expected, the judge, who had seventy-two-hours to act, ruled after the hearing that there was sufficient evidence of the crimes to warrant holding the four suspects for trial.

When reporters noticed bloodstains on Elio's shirt sleeve, and a split lip, he joked that he had punched himself.

But more serious allegations of police torture surfaced a bit later in the proceedings, when an attorney for Martinas Salinas, who is also the defendant's uncle, filed a complaint with a state court judge in the nearby town of Reynosa asking that incriminating statements signed by all four of the suspects be nullified. The complaint claimed that the four suspects were denying knowledge of the murders, although Elio Hernandez Rivera admitted being a member of the cult.

According to the attorney's statement, his nephew was tortured with beatings, electrical shocks, and had a plastic bag pulled over his head seven times until he lost consciousness. One of Martinez's eardrums was burst as a result, it was claimed.

Although Mexican authorities denied the accusations, photographs of the suspects, taken by a doctor who also examined them, appeared to lend some credence to the charges. The photos were taken by Dr. Paulina Vela

---

Esquivel, a professor of medicine at the University Autonoma of Tamaulipas, in Matamoros.

They show broken capillaries in Elio Hernandez's left eye, and tiny red marks that look like pimples on his back and ears. Dr. Vela said the broken capillaries were consistent with damage that could be expected from a lack of oxygen, and that the marks on Elio's back were from electric shocks.

She also told reporters that Serafin Hernandez had fading signs of bruises on his back and upper chest and that some of his ribs were broken. The doctor added that the photos were taken eight days after the alleged torture.

Prosecution of the charges against Elio's older brother, Serafin Hernandez Rivera, the only accused member of the drug trafficking gang to be filed in U.S. courts, was moving more slowly. And the case was also complicated by the accusations of torture.

When Hernandez was indicted, police had neither any confiscated marijuana or other physical evidence positively linking him to a drug smuggling plot. Consequently, near the end of May, an assistant U.S. attorney dropped the charges against him.

But authorities weren't yet ready to give up and release him from the Cameron County Jail in Brownsville where he was being held without bail. Only four days after the old charges were dropped, new charges were filed implicating him in a reputed one-kilogram cocaine deal and the smuggling of 243 pounds of marijuana. He was also named on illegal firearms charges, after police said they found a sawed-off shotgun not registered to him, when they searched his home in Brownsville. He pleaded innocent to the charges, which were based on transactions DEA agents claimed occurred in 1987.

The warrant used by DEA agents to search the man's Brownsville home, as well as confessions by the Matamoros suspects, were challenged in documents filed in U.S. federal court by Hernandez Rivera's lawyer. Attorney Richard Hoffman claimed in the action that American lawmen had watched as Mexican police tortured the prisoners to extract confessions and information used to obtain the search warrant.

The attorney asked Judge Filermon Vela to ban federal prosecutors from using evidence gathered as a result of the search, and from using any information resulting from interrogation by Mexican police of the suspects held in Matamoros. Hoffman especially singled out as damaging, statements by his client's son, Serafin Hernandez Garcia.

Other court documents disclosed that DEA agents who went through the house in Brownsville, questioned the Matamoros suspects in videotaped interviews three days before obtaining the search warrant. In an affidavit by DEA Special Agent T. K. Solis, he wrote that in an interview with Serafin Hernandez Garcia at Federal Judicial Police headquarters in Matamoros, the young suspects said his father had introduced him to the family business trafficking in drugs.

"Hernandez Garcia stated that since arriving in Brownsville, he and his father have supported the family solely with the proceeds of narcotics transactions," the DEA agent declared in the document.

But information used to justify issuing of the search warrant wasn't obtained solely from interrogation of the Matamoros drug and murder suspects. One of the additional sources of information allegedly linking the Hernandez family to drug smuggling was a sister of the younger Serafin. She was quoted in the court documents as saying that other relatives told her that the family income derived "from drug trafficking, and nobody in the family holds legitimate employment." The young woman was quoted as telling the agents that documents tieing the family to the drug business could be found in their Brownsville home.

Hoffman didn't pinpoint the specific U.S. law enforcement officers who allegedly witnessed the torture sessions, and identified them in the motion only as "special agents."

Remarking in his motion that evidence obtained through physical abuse has no place in U.S. courts, Hoffman wrote: "The actions of the police shock the conscience of civilized people and are to be condemned by an ordered society."

Lieutenant Gavito, who had admittedly sat in on various interrogations of the Matamoros suspects, quickly responded with strong denials that he or any other American law enforcement officers he knew of had witnessed torture by Mexican police. In a statement carried by the *Brownsville Herald*, Gavito said he saw no one hit or tortured, but that the suspects were "singing like little birds" anyway.

The sensational motion, along with others requesting that bail be set for the elder Hernandez and that the trial be moved from Brownsville because of the heavy publicity in the local media, were taken under advisement.

Earlier, a judge had granted a petition by an attorney for the forty-five-year-old Brownsville man for a gag order to prevent government officials from discussing charges against him with the press.

One final curious twist in the tangled high-profile case occurred in Miami, when Constanzo's mother, Delia Gonzalez del Valle was sentenced to two years in prison on grand theft charges for stealing a refrigerator from a home where she had been working as a caretaker. She filed an appeal.

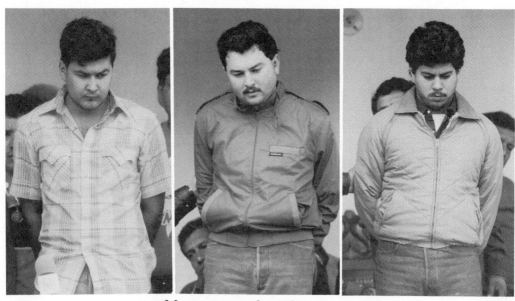

More suspects from the gang.

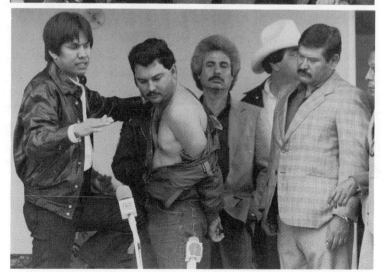

Bringing in more suspects.

Epilogue

THE MEXICAN GOVERNMENT NOW owns the Santa Elena Ranch. The shed is gone and the debris left after it's ritual burning has been cleaned up. Barely three months after the decomposing remains of the men and boys buried there were removed, a field of maize was growing a few yards away.

Presumably the superstitious residents of other nearby ranches, and of Matamoros, are satisfied that the *curandero*'s cleansing and the act of the *federales* in putting the torch to the shed destroyed the source of power of the wicked young man who was variously called *El Cubano, El Padrino,* and Adolfo de Jesus Constanzo.

And there seems to be little doubt that another 200,000 or more college students will flock to South Padre Island for the next Spring Break. Many of them will likely make the added journey to the border and Matamoros. Some will probably be attracted to the city, specifically because of the reluctant notoriety it gained from the atrocities at the Hell Ranch.

Constanzo's legacy of evil will live on. Someday, he and his rapacious band of killers may even be translated into border legend.

Today, however, there is no question about the inimitable evil, pain, and misery inflicted by Constanzo's ruthless bandit clan.

It's true, of course, that residents of the border area and Mexico City who suffered most directly from the blood orgy can breathe a sigh of relief in the knowledge that the nucleus of the drug trafficking cult has been broken up. The men and the woman believed to have made up the core of the leadership are dead, or in police custody. Those who are already behind bars awaiting trial, are expected to be convicted and to remain locked up for many years.

And an international manhunt has been launched for several other suspects of the shattered Hernandez-Constanzo gang whom authorities in the United States or Mexico believe to have been involved in the drug smuggling branch of the operation. Investigators are continuing to interrogate suspects already in custody, as well, and to check out new leads in efforts to track down any of the late *El Padrino*'s former associates who may still be involved in human sacrifice.

But nothing has really changed on the border. Poverty and desperation still exist alongside the rich cultural heritage of the area, the bountiful crop yields of the irrigated Rio Grande Valley, the bustling commerce made possible by the close proximity of good highways, airports, and deep water ports, and a ready supply of efficient labor, as well as forward looking community leaders in the cities of Texas, Tamaulipas, Nuevo Leon, Chihuahua and other Mexican border states.

There has been nothing to indicate that the thriving border trade in drugs and illegal immigrants has slowed by even the slightest since the breakup of Constanzo's gang.

After the first shocked screams of fear and anguish over revelations of the macabre human sacrifice carried out at the ranch, most citizens have settled back into their routine, content to let police, clergymen and other experts deal with the very real threat of black magic cults.

And despite President Salinas's obviously sincere desire to clean up corruption and crack down on drug trafficking in Mexico and on its borders, he is faced with a herculeon job that isn't going to be completed overnight.

Still, advances are being made.

The Kilroys, Mark's parents and younger brother not only showed great courage and faith throughout their ordeal, but responded to the tragedy by doing everything they could to mobilize a fresh new grassroots drive against narcotics trafficking and drug abuse. They insistently point out that although their son wasn't a drug user, others who use drugs must share the responsibility for the loss of his life.

James Kilroy told reporters that people who say using a little marijuana doesn't hurt anyone, are wrong. "It killed my son," he said. He is correct. If there is no demand for a product, there is no need for supply.

In memory of their son, the Kilroys established an anti-drug foundation called, Make A Responsible Kommitment, or MARK. Based in their hometown of Santa Fe, Texas, the organization was formulated to pressure public officials to crack down harder on drugs. As one of their first steps, the family hoped to obtain five million signatures to put the federal government on notice that Americans are demanding an effective anti-drug policy. Plans called for presenting the petition to William Bennett, the Bush Administration's drug czar.

James Kilroy took a leave of absence from his job as a chemical engineer to lead the crusade. He and his wife, Helen, travelled through Texas and other states to spread the word about their drive against drugs. Three objectives of the effort to influence formation of the national drug policy include eliminating pushers, stopping the so-called recreational use of drugs among those not already addicted, and providing rehabilitation for those already hooked.

At a news conference with legislators, prosecutors and police in Austin, the Texas state capitol, the Kilroys called for a military role in the war against drugs to include the use of abandoned bases staffed by U.S. troops in which to confine drug dealers. They also recommended mandatory prison terms, grants to local law enforcement agencies, and cash rewards for citizens who help in the arrest of drug dealers.

"This is really a war we're in," said James Kilroy. "Two years ago, if we had united and done this, I believe Mark would still be with us today."

The Kilroys planned to establish a medical school scholarship in their son's name, with money from a trust fund already set up.

But perhaps the most shining contribution to the neighbors of the Kilroys was their stoic, quiet faith, and the example they provided for others in the manner in which they dealt with their personal tragedy.

And Mark, young Jose Luis Garcia Luna, and other innocents who died at the Hell Ranch left their own unforgettable legacy to their survivors. Their unwilling sacrifice focused public and private attention on the out-of-control drug war that is raging on the U.S.-Mexican border.

Although their meeting was scheduled before the discovery of the cult killings in Matamoros, nearly 100 law officers from Texas and U.S. federal agencies, and authorities from the Mexican states of Tamaulipas, Nuevo Leon, Coahuila and Chihuahua gathered in the town of Pharr for a one-day border law enforcement conference. Officials stated that the horrific crimes committed by the Constanzo gang gave the conference special urgency.

With interpreters providing Spanish and English translations, the law officers discussed and planned improved methods of communication between border agencies in efforts to upgrade the crime fighting abilities of police on both sides of the Rio Grande. Texas State Attorney General Jim Mattox co-hosted the one-day meet.

Texas lawmen were already pleased with the extraordinary level of cooperation by state and federal authorities in Mexico during investigation of the Mark Kilroy abduction, the drug smuggling crimes and murders. Gavito was especially generous in his praise of Commandante Benitez and other Mexican lawmen for their unprecedented spirit of cooperation. Among his observations, Gavito noted that when he was asked to testify for the prosecution in Matamoros about the gang's drug trafficking activities it marked the first time he had ever heard of an American lawman being given such an invitation by Mexico.

At another higher level meeting, U.S. Attorney General Richard Thornburg met with Mexico Attorney General Enrique Alvarez del Castillo, to lay the groundwork for establishing closer ties and smoother relationships between government and police agencies in the joint war on drugs. Among the specific proposals were plans for working on joint interdiction operations, for

U.S. assistance in the training of Mexican police and drug enforcement agents, and study of schemes for increasing cross-border cooperation, seizing the assets of proven drug traffickers, and updating the extradition treaty between the two nations.

On yet another front, Texas legislators were quick to introduce bills in Congress calling for special investigations of drug abuse and black magic cults. Rep. Solomon Ortiz, a Corpus Christi Democrat, suggested the probe might be conducted by a joint committee of U.S. and Mexican officials. Ortiz, who is a member of the House Committee on Narcotics Abuse and Control, said he expected his own group to look into the problem.

The Texas House and Senate were also asked in twin bills to create a special category of crimes in the state penal code to cover cult-related behavior that includes the ritualistic drinking of blood, or cannibalism. The Republican co-sponsors, Senator J. E. "Buster" Brown, of Lake Jackson, and Representative Sam Johnson, of Plano, warned that the problem of blood cults was burgeoning in Texas and that law enforcement officers had urged them to adopt strong new laws to crack down on ritualistic crime.

But the growing problem of cult related crime is a problem that must be addressed on other levels. Legislation and laws alone will not provide all the answers.

Police departments throughout the country have already equipped themselves with specially trained officers, or are training specialists to probe cult crimes. Others call on civilian experts, individuals and organizations, who offer their own special expertise to help in the investigation of ritual murders, animal mutilation, and child abuse that appear to be tied to cult activities. Clergymen in churches and synagogues have added their warnings to the dangers of blood cults and the lure of dangerous occultism to the young.

But it is difficult to legislate against religious practices, even those that call for the blood sacrifice of animals. And there is a legitimate danger of trampling on the rights of believers in religious sects that are merely out of step with the more traditional faiths of mainstream Anglo America. In Hialeah, Florida, Constanzo's former home, a stubborn young *Santero* priest is fighting a court battle for the right to practice his religion openly in a church.

Supported by the American Civil Liberties Union, Ernesto Pichardo, found himself pitted against powerful forces in the community and a trio of city ordinances that banned the ritual killing of animals. In *Santeria*, animals are sacrificed and herbs and fruits are offered to summon the gods. His attorneys have compared the ritual killing of animals in *Santeria* ceremonies with the kosher killing of animals for food by some of the Jewish faith. The animals are slain cleanly, with sure, swift strokes of the knife. And their flesh is later consumed at meals or feasts.

The *Santeria* god, "Babalu-Aye" is the spiritual alter-ego of St. Lazarus, patron saint of the sick. *Santeros* in Florida, Louisiana, New York, Illinois, and other states where the religion has gained a strong foothold were horrified by the tragedy at Matamoros, and firmly deny that their faith has anything to do with human sacrifice.

There are real devils, and frightening blood cultists devoted to human sacrifice, degradation, and terror to ferret out, without seeking innocent scapegoats among legitimate practitioners of *Santeria.*

Worshipping Satan isn't against the law. But Satanic cultists do kill. There have been unsettling reports of a killer cult of (the Hindu goddess) Kali kidnapping and performing human sacrifices on the West Coast, as well. And like Constanzo, young people especially, sometimes formulate their own bastard rituals from a weird melange of underground religions and curious cults that lead them to animal mutilation, suicide or homicide.

And black magic, Satanism, and some other more negative cult practices have definitely worked their way into the drug culture and narcotics smuggling world. It is a partnership formed in Hell.

But the real problem that must be solved to prevent another Hell Ranch, is stopping the unbridled drug trade. The deceitful lure of narco-dollars has turned the border into a battlefield, and poses unique troubles that both Mexico and the United States must work together to solve. Our cities are being overrun by drug dealers and junkies, who prey on other criminals and law abiding citizens as well.

The cunning use of exotic, foreign religious rites tangled and manipulated by crime kingpins to instill fear and maintain discipline among their rank and file, is merely the latest devilish twist in the conundrum. Cultism has soiled the already dirty business of drugs and turned it into a repulsive blood feast.

Neither more education about the dangers of drug abuse, nor more treatment facilities will solve the problem. And there is no longer time nor acceptable excuses for revolving door justice for people involved in the drug trade. Only the promise of swift and ruthlessly sure retribution, with execution or mandatory prison terms for drug smugglers and dealers, will equip decent Americans with the muscle to win the battle against the purveyors of poison. If the National Guard or the Army has to be called on to round up or engage the drug traffickers in firefights, they should be mobilized. Our nation is at war!

A Texas state official has called for a law enforcement blitzkrieg against the narcotics trade. We should take his advice and act. It's time to get tough!